MODERN TEACHING OF CIVICS/POLITICAL SCIENCE

Modern Teaching of Civics/Political Science

[Strictly According to the UGC Syllabus for B.Ed. Course]

By
M.H. SYED

ANMOL PUBLICATIONS PVT. LTD.
NEW DELHI - 110 002 (INDIA)

ANMOL PUBLICATIONS PVT. LTD.
4374/4B, Ansari Road, Daryaganj
New Delhi - 110 002
Ph.: 23261597, 23278000
Visit us at: www.anmolpublications.com

Modern Teaching of Civics/Political Science

First Published, 2004

ISBN 81-261-1868-7

PRINTED IN INDIA

Published by J.L. Kumar for Anmol Publications Pvt. Ltd., New Delhi - 110 002 and Printed at Mehra Offset Press, Delhi.

Contents

Preface

Education is a vast discipline and Teachers' Training is a vital part of it. The responsibilities of the educationists and educators are focused on the task of providing better training to the future teachers for their better learning and proper development. Needless to say that this responsibility can only be exercised, if the trainers are equipped with the required knowledge of the subject concerned. That's why it becomes essential for making adequate provisions for each course to the student-teachers or teacher trainees. The present series is designed for providing a solid workable base for all course-papers. It has been prepared strictly according to the syllabus of the B.Ed class, prescribed by the UGC for different universities.

No doubt, there are so many other books on the subject, available in the market, written by worthy authors. However, every writer has his or her own style and way of presentation. The present work also has its own features and characteristics.

In preparation of this series of texts, the editor had to refer to the works of other authors and information sources. The editor feels a deep sense of gratitude for incorporating their ideas in the text. Hopefully, this series would serve as a 'ready to refer' tool for all teachers, teacher-students and others.

— Editor

1
Introduction

"The outstanding purpose of instruction in Civics is to produce citizens and to aid pupils in the formation of a higher type of civic character."

For several centuries, India had to suffer under the yoke of subjugation. The citizens of a slave country the Indians were deprived of the right of citizenship. Their qualities were not allowed to be developed. After Independence, the situation has changed altogether. India has declared itself a Sovereign Democratic Republic. Citizens have a special position in a democratic country. Without conscious and educated citizens, democracy cannot function effectively. The entire burden of administration rests on the citizens. The citizens too have become conscious of their duties and obligations. The study of civics is necessary in order to develop the qualities of citizenship. Without the proper study of civics it is not possible for the citizens to know and understand their rights and obligations.

On account of its importance for the citizens of a democratic country Civics must find a suitable place in the curriculum of studies. It should have a privileged position, which it has yet to achieve. Formerly, in lower classes, specially up to Junior High Schools, Civics was taught as a part of social studies along with History and Geography. Today, it is being taught as a separate subject.

Teaching Aims and Objectives

No subject can be taught effectively unless the teacher is well aware and conscious of its aims and objectives along with the capacity to modify these aims and objectives, according to the requirements of the society as the aims and objectives cannot remain the same in all times and under all circumstances. The teacher should utilise these aims and objectives to produce ideal citizens of the country.

Ideal Citizenship, the main aim of civics: The most important aim of teaching Civics is to produce ideal citizens. Young men and women that come out of the educational institutions should have all the qualities of a successful citizen of a democratic country. They should have a democratic outlook. They should be fully conscious of their rights, duties and obligations. They should be prepared to play their part in the development of the society. If they play their role effectively, the country is bound to progress by leaps and bounds. They should be guided by the ideal of 'Live and Let Live'. These things can be taught only by Civics.

A democracy can succeed only if the citizens of that country are ideal and prepared to face the challenging responsibilities that have been put on them. Democracy requires intellectual, social and other qualities that can grow only with the help of Civics. In the words of H. H. Home "Citizenship is a man's place in the State. As the State is one of the permanent institutions of society and as man must ever live in organized relations with his fellows, citizenship cannot be omitted from the constituency of the educational ideal." Civics is the subject that deals with every thing appertaining to citizenships, past, present and future, local; national and human. The teacher should aim at inculcating these virtues in the young citizens of motherland.

As ancient Greek philosophers recognised, ideal citizenship is the main aim of the Civics. It was said in the 'Civic Oath':

"We will never bring disgrace to this our city by any act of dishonesty or cowardice, nor desert our suffering comrades. We will fight for the ideals and sacred things of the city, alone and with many; we will revere and obey the city's laws and do our best to incite alike respect in those among us who are prone to annul them or set them at naught ; we will strive unceasingly to quicken the public sense of civic thought. Thus, in all these ways we will transmit this city and not only not less, but greater, better, more beautiful than it was transmitted to us."

Recognising this fact the Secondary Education Commission appointed by the Government of India wrote in its report:

"To be effective, a democratic citizen should have the understanding and the intellectual integrity to sift truth from falsehood, facts from propaganda, to reject the dangerous appeal of fanaticism and prejudice. He must develop a scientific attitude of mind to think objectively and base his conclusions on tested data. He should have an open mind receptive to new ideas and not confined within prison walls of out-moded customs, traditions and beliefs. He should neither reject the old because it is old nor accept the new because it is new, but dispassionately examine both and courageously reject whatever arrests the forces of justice and progress."

Development of civic-character: Teaching of Civics aims at producing citizens endowed with ideal civic-character. Having full knowledge of the administrative set up of the country they should be prepared to play their part as citizens of a Sovereign Democratic Republic.

National character and patriotism: No country can progress effectively unless its citizens are imbued in the spirit of patriotism. Indians should be prepared to sacrifice everything for their motherland. They should also be proud of their cultural heritage and uphold the values of the society. These traits can be inculcated only if the teacher of Civics tries to handle pupils at their impressionable age, in a psychological and scientific manner. He should try to develop national character by basing it on the virtues of co-operation, love, sympathy, etc.

Education for democracy: The objective of education in India is to try to achieve the aims laid down in the Constitution. A democratic nation aims at instilling a love of liberty, equality and fraternity in its people. And, if India is to be made a truly democratic nation, education should aim at developing these qualities. Hence, education aims at the total and independent development of the individual. But in this development it is essential that personal liberty should be in consonance with social justice. Social justice is based on equality. It provides every citizen with the opportunity to pursue his own development without prejudicing the interests of others. One implication is that the government must provide the poor people with the opportunity and the help to get an education which will raise them to the same level as the others, because without this help they cannot secure such education for themselves. And without it, equality will have no meaning.

The most important democratic objective and ideal of education is the evolution of the sense of fraternity because democratic life is impossible without it. This feeling of brotherhood makes little of the differences generated by caste, race, class, profession, sex, nation, etc. and gives rise to a genuine love of humanity and human beings. The future of any democracy depends entirely upon its future citizens and the quality of leadership. Hence, one of the important functions of education is that it should train the educands in democratic leadership. It is a truism that students are the future leaders of the nation. Education, therefore, must evolve ways and means of training these prospective leaders in the norms of democratic life. For this, it is essential that the student community itself must evolve a democratic pattern, and it must be burdened with much of the responsibilities of running the educational institutions in order to get practical training in social living.

This education for democracy can be given only through the teaching of civics as a compulsory subject.

Citizenship Education: Accepting citizenship as one of the major aims of education is of particular importance for democratic nations. If a dictatorial system of government prevails in a country, then training in citizenship is not very significant because in such a country, the citizens play a very small role in the administration of the country. On the other hand, democratic countries depend upon their masses for development in every sphere, and it is no exaggeration to say that success or failure of the country depends upon the citizens. Bertrand Russell astutely observed that democracy should not even be thought of in a country in which the masses are uneducated. If democracy is to be a success, it is essential that the people of the country be educated in responsible citizenship. It must be remembered that the training in citizenship is provided not so much by schools and other educational institutions as much as by lectures, radio, television, newspapers and institutions of self-government. Even the different political parties can make a lot of positive contribution in this direction.

Again, the foregoing description should not lead to the belief that training for citizenship is required only in a democracy and it is superfluous in other forms of government such as dictatorship, fascism or communism. It is true that in societies of this kind, the citizens are not called upon to share in the responsibilities of government as much as in a democratic set up, but even here some training in citizenship is essential. There is a difference between democratic citizenship and citizenship in these forms of governments. For example, communist governments do not encourage their citizens to think much because the average citizen there does not have the right to raise his voice against his government.

Education for Citizenship

In order to fully comprehend training in citizenship as an important objective of Civics it is essential to understand the qualities and abilities that such an education must seek to generate in the educand. Some important aspects are the following

General knowledge of the various problems of individual and social life. Man's life, whether personal or social, is beset with various kinds of problems in all its aspects and forms such as the economic, political, moral, spiritual, physiological, mental, etc. Education should aim at equipping the individual with some general knowledge regarding all these problems so that he may not have any extraordinary difficulty in facing them. General knowledge in itself is important in democratic countries, because the individual citizens are expected to help in the progress of the country in every sphere. .

Socialization. Socialization is the prerequisite for evolving the qualities of responsible citizenship. In the absence of socialization the individual cannot fulfil his responsibilities as a citizen. In fact, he has little obligation to discharge his duties in the first place. After the home, the college or the university is the next important medium of socialization. Here various programmes can be organised to develop such qualities as mutual cooperation, friendship, social service, sacrifice, sympathy, etc. These help in individual's socialization and thus prepare him for the role of the citizen.

Total development. Every democratic nation must provide for the comprehensive development of its masses if it wants ideal citizens. Hence, education should aim at the all round development of the child, his physical, mental, moral, spiritual development. Only then can they be expected to devote themselves to the task of serving their nation, and making an honest contribution to the nation's economic and spiritual progress.

Fulfilment of political responsibility. Only he is a good citizen who honestly and zealously fulfils his political responsibility along with the other obligations he has to society, For example, in an election, it is the duty of every adult man and woman to elect the best possible candidate to represent the electorate, so that the country may get the best leaders. Citizens should be aware of their responsibilities, be prepared to defend their rights and be willing to fulfil their obligations. Every individual must learn to think independently. As Walker has commented, education in a democracy does not imply that the individual should become a tool of the government. He has himself to be an administrator or prepare others for this role. Hence, individuals must be trained to become leaders themselves and also to elect leaders.

Creation of political consciousness and social efficiency. Teaching of Civics aims at generating political consciousness in the students and also make them socially efficient. They should be well aware of the political and social problems of the country. They should try to take active part in them. The future of the country depends on the students of today. Social efficiency requires that the young men should have the qualities of sympathy, co-operation, patriotism, etc. All these values are imbibed if the study of Civics is carried out in a scientific manner.

Consciousness of rights and duties. In Civics, students study the ways of exercising their rights, to grow and become noble and useful members of the group. They learn performing their duties, in order to help others to exercise their rights.

Development of mental powers. Every subject aims at the development of certain mental powers of the students such as, imagination, reasoning, power of criticism, firmness of determination, etc. Being a social science Civics has to perform this task more effectively. It aims at development of the mental powers of the students in a successful manner. Unless these mental powers are developed the students shall not be able to grow into successful citizens.

Scientific outlook. Ours is an age of science. Every man should have a scientific outlook. Scientific outlook is looking at things in proper perspective. Civics aim at development of scientific outlook in the students. It helps them to leave unscientific and un-necessary things in their life.

Cosmopolitan outlook. Today with the development of science and technology, the barriers of time and space are crumbling down. It is not far off, when the entire world shall be knit in one single unit. No citizen of a country can keep himself away from the ways of other countries. A man can be a real citizen of his country only if he has a cosmopolitan outlook. It is the cosmopolitan outlook, which will lead him to acquire the attitude of 'Co-existence' or the principle of 'Live and Let Live'. The teacher of Civics should aim at teaching cosmopolitanism.

View of Adam Wesley. Adam Wesley has laid down the following aims and objectives of the teaching of Civics :

Government. The teaching of civics should aim at making students capable of understanding the needs and requirements of the Government and its structure.

Political parties. It should aim at acquainting students with the activities and formation of the political parties.

Democracy. It should strengthen the faith of the young citizens in democracy and teach them the value of co-operation among the States.

Rights and duties. At the State level, it, should acquaint the citizens with their rights and duties and enable the students to play an active part in the solution of the, political problems. It is natural that they shall not be able to play their part, unless they are able to understand them.

Human welfare. The teaching of Civics should aim at strengthening the feelings of human-welfare, world-peace, public-good, etc. in the students.

Democrative traits. Spirit of co-operation, sympathy, love, etc., should be developed in the students. These qualities will enable them to discharge their obligations, as citizens, successfully.

QUESTIONS

1. In what way has the value of teaching Civics in schools increased with the achievement of independence? How should this teaching be different from what it was in pre-independence days?
2. Bring out clearly the importance of teaching of Civics and also show the aims and values of its teaching.
3. What are the aims and objects of teaching Civics as a subject at the higher secondary stage ?

2
The Fundamentals

A branch of Social Science, Civics, is as old as the human civilisation. It is part of the Political Science. Prior to its recognition as a separate subject, it was taught along with History and Political Science. This subject found place in the curriculum only in the nineteenth century due to the lack of consciousness on the part of the people.

Importance of the Subject

As a subject the importance of Civics lies in its utility to the society. It recognizes man as a social animal. Civics studies him accordingly. Really speaking , the man has certain basic instincts. Gregariousness is one such instinct. Due to this instinct, man wants to live in groups. Society came into being as a result of this instinct. Therefore a man cannot develop without realising the interest of the society and its different organs and parts.

While, man tries to adjust to the circumstances in which he is placed, he tries to acquire supremacy over the physical and social factors. His attempt to acquire supremacy has brought about the evolution of different branches of knowledge. As a result of man's desire to acquire supremacy over social forces Civics came into being. In the beginning, Civics was only a form of social studies, an integrated subject combining History, Civics, Geography, etc. As Civics acquired an independent status, it is recognised as a social science.

Only in a well organised society, it is possible for a man to make unhampered progress. Man has been trying to establish his superiority over other living beings since time immemorial. It is the society that enabled him to achieve the talents and the qualities through which he could make progress and achieve superiority over other living beings.

While man tries to establish his superiority over other living being, he also makes efforts to resolve conflicts and live in harmony with other social beings. He looks after the interests and requirements of his other fellow beings. Co-existence is the ideal of his social life. It is here that the need of the study of the Civics comes in. Through the knowledge of Civics, it is possible for a man to learn about the co-operation that he has to establish with his other fellow beings. As a social science Civics tries to resolve social conflict in the society and help man to live in harmony with his other fellow beings.

The Origin

The word 'Civics' has been derived from the Latin word 'Civic' which means 'a citizen'. The Latin- 'Civitas' means a City State. Both these words have given birth to the social science called 'Civics'.

In olden days, Greece and Rome were two great States in Europe. They tried to govern the various affairs with the help of a set system of rules. These rules were framed by the citizens of those States. They called their small city states 'Civitas'. While enjoying political and social rights the citizens also had to discharge social and political obligations. As the population of city-states grew the city-states were converted into big empires. However, even these big empires were called 'Civitas'. Later on the words 'Civic' and 'Civitas' were adopted in English language and the words 'Citizen', 'City' and state came into being.

With the growth of the human culture and civilization, man assumed the role of the leader of the society. He was termed as the 'crown of the creation'. He started assessing and evaluating the knowledge of various subjects with his intellect and intelligence. In the twentieth century while the context and the content remained more or less the same, 'Civics', 'Civic' and 'Civitas' changed in context though the meanings that they denoted and connoted in the olden days lingered on.

Today as the barriers of space and time have ceased to exist, the world is in the process of being linked together in one single unit. With this change in social conditions the outlook of human beings has changed. A need for world-fraternity has grown all over the world. Hence Civics has assumed greater importance.

Meaning and Definition

1. In his famous book *The Philosophy of Citizenship,* Dr. E.M. White defines Civics in the following words. "Civics is that more or less useful branch of human knowledge, which deals with every thing (social, intellectual, economical, political and even religious aspects) appertaining to citizenship, past, present and future, local, national, international and human. Civics is that branch of knowledge which deals with all the aspects of social life of a citizen. His local, national and international needs are studied under this social science."

With the study of civics men become acquainted with all the aspects of the life of a citizen. Civics tells us what the man originally was and what he has become today. Laying stress on the social aspect of the life of the citizen Dr. Beni Prasad has defined civics in the following words- "In the context of, social relationship, there are many duties to be performed and correspondingly many rights are to be respected. It is with them that civics is mainly concerned."

Civics, is the science and philosophy of citizenship. It tells the individuals about their rights and duties and the things that they are supposed to do.

In the words of F. J. Gould "Civics is the study of institutions, habits and spirit by means of which a man or a woman may fulfil the duties and receive the benefits of membership in a political community."

A. T. Shah. "Civics may be defined as that branch of human knowledge which deals with rights and duties of man living as a member of a group of people politically organized."

Oxford Dictionary. "Civics is the theory of rights and duties of citizenship."

All these definitions very clearly bring out the fact that Civics is the study of the various facets of the citizen's life.

A Social Science

Some scholars are of the view that civics is not a science. They have in their mind the picture of the physical sciences. Sciences are of two kinds, (a) Physical, and (b) Social Science.

In Physical Science there is a rigidity of rule with the result that two and two definitely make four at every place and in every situation. In Social Science it is not so. Social sciences have their own rules. They also follow the methodology of science in observation, collection of the data, its classification and laying down of theories, etc., but these theories are not very mathematical and rigid. They change with the change in socio-economic conditions.

Lord Bryce has remarked that Civics or Political Science is as good a science as astronomy. We can not have only conjectures in Civics. We have to base the knowledge on solid foundations. Civics science studies the interests, aptitudes, rights and duties and other aspects of the social life of the citizen. These are studied in a scientific and systematized manner. From the point of view of science, it may be stated that Civics is a systematized body of knowledge that deals with citizenship.

Comparison

Social Science	*Physical Sciences*
1. Social sciences investigate laws related to man or man's social behaviour.	1. The physical sciences search for physical laws in natural phenomena.
2. Social sciences proceed upon the assumption that man is the central figure in the world.	2. There is no equivalent in physical sciences.
3. The fundamental elements of social sciences are psychologically related.	3. The basic elements of physical sciences are physically related.

Social sciences	Physical sciences
4. The basic elements of social sciences are men, their mental states and behaviour.	4. The basic elements of the physical sciences are the physical elements like hydrogen, etc.
5. The basic elements of the social sciences cannot be separated analytically.	5. The basic elements of the physical sciences can be separated by analysis.
6. Being related to the study of society the social sciences have comparatively less exactness.	6. Because they study physical elements the physical sciences possess greater exactness.
7. Because of their lesser exactness, social sciences can make comparatively fewer predictions.	7. The physical sciences can make more predictions due to a higher degree of exactness.
8. For this reason objectivity is achieved with difficulty in social sciences.	8. Objectivity is attained easily in physical sciences.
9. Social sciences provide comparatively lesser scope for measurement of subject matter.	9. There is greater possibility of measurement in the study of physical phenomena.
10. It is difficult to construct laboratories for social sciences. Society is their laboratory.	10. Physical sciences have their own laboratories because they can easily be established for studying physical objects.

It is a Social Science

Considering the differences between social sciences and physical sciences in respect of their view points, subject matter and theory, etc., it becomes evident that in calling civics a science, one does not mean to accord to it the same degree of exactness as that found in the physical sciences. Civics can lay claim to being a science because it employs the scientific method in its study. Its exactness, the capacity to predict, the possibility of measurement in it, etc., are comparatively, less than the physical sciences, in view of its unique subject matter. Despite these factors, it can be called a science just as a number of other sciences are so called in spite of all these drawbacks. The examples are psychology, astronomy, etc.

As an Art

Some social scientists believe that civics is only an art. Art is the practical application of the knowledge acquired by the science. From this point of view, Civics is an art. It is not satisfied with collection of the knowledge about citizenship in a systematic manner. It tries to put that knowledge into practice. It tries to solve the question- Who is an ideal citizen? What is an ideal citizenship? What is a successful social life? In a practical manner, it also inspires people to put the knowledge in the practical form. In short, Civics is a science as well as an art. Stressing on this point Dr. Beni Prasad has defined Civics in the following words, "Civics is both science and art in the sense that it investigates conditions and seeks to apply the results of its investigations to the furtherance of human welfare."

Place in the Curriculum

A good deal of controversy has been waged about providing a place to civics in the syllabus. Some scholars believe that it is a very important social science and it should find a place in the curriculum, others who do not agree with it, say that the subject-matter of civics is found in other social sciences as well and so it shall be of no practical use to make the students study it. This theory is not acceptable to modern educationists. They believe that Civics must find a place in the curriculum, because it teaches us the rules and regulations of ideal citizenship and also encourages people to put them into practice. It is not only a theoretical science. The following arguments have advanced in favour of giving a place to Civics in the curriculum:-

Knowledge of citizenship. Students of today shall be the citizens of tomorrow. They should know their rights and obligations as citizens. Only the study of Civics can teach them about it.

Cooperation and coexistence. Co-operation and co-existence are essential for a successful social life. These elements lead human society to a real progress. The study of Civics can teach young minds of these virtues and values.

Education for democracy. India is a democratic country. Political consciousness is a fundamental requirement of democracy. To arouse it, it is very necessary to have political and social consciousness in young men. As it can be achieved through the study of Civics, so civics should find a place in the curriculum.

Study of obligations. All young men and women should be taught the art of successful living. They cannot live successfully unless they have an idea of the obligations of a social being. It is the study of Civics that imparts knowledge of this to them.

Teaching of administration. Successful administration of a country depends upon its citizens. Young men and women can be administrators only if they are taught the art of administration during their student life. Study of Civics helps them in this direction.

International understanding. Our's is an age of internationalism. Nationalism has also to flourish along with internationalism. An attempt should be made to make nationalism and inter-nationalism co-exist. Study of Civics can help young men and woman in this direction as well.

Scientific outlook. It is very necessary to have a scientific outlook in the students. Study of Civics helps them to acquire this scientific outlook.

Place in National Educational System

National and secular outlook. In India Civics as a subject has special importance in the national educational system. Through Civics, it is possible to create a broad national and secular outlook. To quote the report of the Secondary Education Commission presided over by Dr. Mudaliar: "The education system must make its contribution to the development of habits, attitudes and qualities of character, which will enable its citizens to bear worthily the responsibilities of democratic citizenship and to counteract all those fissiparous tendencies which hinder the emergence of a broad national and secular outlook."

Education for citizenship. As a subject that teaches us about citizenship, Civics has its place in the national educational system of India. It can be possible to develop ideal citizens through the teaching of Civics. As Patric Geddes has remarked, "Civics is the youngest and last branch of science as yet but a little noticed fruit on the vast and ever spreading tree of knowledge which may be recognized as one of the most fruitful of all" the Words of Bining and Bining "The outstanding purpose of instruction in Civics is to produce better citizens and to aid pupils in the formation of a higher type of civic character."

Education for democracy. India is a democracy. In a democratic set up, the vote has a lot of value. Voting can succeed only if the citizens know the value of vote and the value of exercising it properly. This can be done only through the teaching of Civics. In a democracy, it is anything more than the thoughtless exercise of the vote, an individual must form his own independent judgement on all kinds of complicated social, economic and political issues and, to a large extent, decide his own course of action. Teaching of Civics can do it to a great extent.

Eradicating of social evils. India's slavery brought in its wake several social evils which have left their reminiscent even in free India. Through the teaching of Civics, it is possible to do away with these social evils.

Interesting and Scientific Manner

Against making the teaching of Civics as a compulsory subject it is said that the teaching of Civics is not interesting to the students. Those who plead for making Civics a compulsory subject, say that it can train the Indian youth in the art of ideal citizenship, while those who oppose its compulsory teaching say that the students get bored after studying this subject. In order to meet this objection, it is necessary to make the teaching of Civics interesting and scientific. Civics should not be taught in the traditional and old manner. Attempt should be made to make its study interesting and scientific.

QUESTIONS

1. Define the term 'Civics'. Is it a science or an art? Discuss its importance in the national educational system?
2. What is Civics? Argue in its favour or against whether it a science or an art.
3. Differentiate between physical and social science and show how civics is a social science.
4. Give arguments to plead why civics should be given a place in modern curriculum.

3
Teaching Methods–I

According to Secondary Education Commission "Even the best curriculum and the most perfect syllabus remains dead unless quickened into life by the right methods of teaching and the right kind of teachers." Method is the means of teaching predetermined ends. It forms the most important link in the total teaching-learning chain with the goals and purposes on the one hand and results and values on the other. Method is the middle link connecting in the objectives with its value. Method determines the quality of result.

All decisions regarding teaching procedures in civics should be governed by the objectives of teaching. The objectives are the specific goals or purposes of a particular unit as well as the nature of the content area of the unit. These would largely determine the methods to be used in teaching or dealing with the unit. In order to achieve the objectives of teaching civics, methods are needed to expose the pupils to knowledge and experiences helpful in the development of understanding, critical thinking, practical skills and interests. The procedures adopted should also provide training in constructive thinking, reasoning and critical judgment. The goal expectations in the teaching of civics involve deeper and extensive participation of students in learning. Hence lecture or merely question answer method would not be adequate. If comprehensive objectives of teaching civics are to be realised in students, there should be child exposed to a variety of learning experiences involving book learning, observation, interviewing, surveying, interpreting, reviewing, recording, reporting and evaluating. The need to make him an enlightened, discriminating, dynamic, productive and democratic citizen would make it imperative to provide him learning experiences geared to that end.

Variety of Methods

The civics teacher must be conversant with the theory and practices of different methods of teaching the subject due to mainly, two reasons :

There is no royal road to successful learning. The teacher should be able to use a permutation and combination of methods, devices, and techniques to make the 'subject interesting, vital and living. He may use lecture or discussion method or a combination of these two, to lend colour to class-teaching. The teacher should be conversant with a variety of methods of teaching civics.

Avoiding monotony: If a teacher uses the same methods-lecture or text-book, project, discussion or socialised recitation in every circumstance it becomes monotonous. In the past few decades a tremendous increase in equipment, materials, means and teaching procedures has been witnessed to provide variety and colour to civics teaching. Children should be exposed to varied experiences to create and maintain their interest and avoid monotony.

No single method is the best for all situations, and with all teachers and pupils. The method of teaching civics should emerge out of the abundance of information and skill of the teacher and should harmonise with the content to be taught. This requires every teacher of civics to be familiar with the different means for reckoning the desired ends.

The Characteristics

Producing change in behaviour: Arranged on an individual as well as group basis, it should provide a group of related experiences and activities specially designed to produce certain changes in terms of knowledge; understanding, habits, attitudes and skills of the students.

Creative expression: It should give scope for the creative expression of the child's individuality.

Arousing interest: Rather than be a mechanical device for passing on facts and figures it should arouse a large range of interests in the minds of the students.

Shift in emphasis: It should shift emphasis from verbalism and memorisation to learning through purposeful, concrete and realistic situations.

Self study and knowledge: It should train the students in the techniques of self-study and the methods of acquiring knowledge through personal effort or intuition.

Stimulating: It should stimulate the desire for further study and exploration.

Awakening insight: It should awaken an insight in the materials and techniques used by a successful civics teacher. It should enable students to know the varied interpretations of events and clash of characters.

Various Methods

Corresponding to the different aims of teaching civics there are the following different methods of teaching civics which the teachers may use according to the needs of a situation.

Story Telling Method

Story telling is one of the most important methods of teaching civics. Stories of great men and women, story of early man, stories of famous rulers, reformers, writers, saints, discoverers and scientists, stories of ideal citizens, all should be told to the children in the primary classes. Narration is an art which aims at presenting to the pupils ordered sequence of events in such a way that their minds are able to reconstruct these happenings and live in imagination through the experiences recounted, either as spectators or possibly as participators. As an actor and speaker, the teacher's capacity can make the lessons lively and interesting to the pupils. They can almost visualise the events and personalities described before their eyes.

For lending colour to personalities and events varied types of stories as myths, legends, moral fables and true historical tales can be used. The type of stories and the manner of their narration will vary with the age of children.

Upto class V, the method of teaching civics should be mainly the story method. Stories and anecdotes enliven the subject matter. Telling of related stories will make the subject matter interesting and lively, even while using other methods as Lecture or Conversation Method or even Discussion and Problem Method.

The Advantages

Satisfies curiosity: Children have an inborn curiosity to learn about various objects and people. The educator can take advantage of this curiosity to tell the children many things through the medium of the story.

Interesting: There are very few people who object to listening to stories. Children in particular enjoy being told stories and hence a story can be used as an interesting medium of education.

Assists memory: It is always easier to remember a subject one finds interesting. Hence, things taught by a story are remembered more easily.

Entertaining: For children, education must also be entertaining, and this is possible only through story telling. This makes the child enjoy his education.

Inspiring. By the use of selected, good and psychological stories much can be done for developing the child's personality and character because stories are stimulating and inspiring.

Development of character: Moral education cannot be given in sermons. It is better, and more effective to tell inspiring stories to the child so that he is presented with a good example which he may strive to follow.

Successful Story-Telling

In order to take advantage of the technique of story-telling, it is essential to present it psychologically, and, in any case, story-telling is an art, albeit an art which can be acquired through practice. The more important factors in successful story-telling are the following

Identification with the story: The more the teacher can forget himself in telling the story, the better it will be. But this is possible only when he himself finds the story interesting. For this reason, it is advisable that the educator should tell only those stories which first interest him.

Sufficient knowledge: Only that story can be powerful and impressive which the educator remembers in all its details. But the story must be told in the educator's own words. It should never be read out, because this is the surest way of boring the audience.

Dramatic presentation: In presenting the story, the educator should enact the various expressions and emotions-described in the story and carry out the actions and gestures which are a part of it. This creates concrete picture in the child's mind and helps him to remember the story.

Adequate language: The language used in telling the story should be simple and within the comprehension of the audience.

Interesting style: The style of story-telling should be natural, life-like, interesting and varied.

Systematic presentation: A systematic presentation and proper ordering of sequences is absolutely essential. If the educator forgets some part and returns to it later on, after having described some future event, the educands are likely to lose the thread and become irritated. Hence, the educator must remember the sequences of events very clearly.

Confirming-to the mental level: Different kinds of stories interest children of different ages. Very young children are usually interested in stories of magic and adventure, stories which are awe-inspiring.

Adolescents find such stories disgusting. But in all such stories, action should be the main element, although the stories are to be selected according to the age group of the audience.

Purposeful: In telling the story, the educator must always keep in mind its purpose. If this is not done, then the purpose will remain unfulfiled.

Necessary atmosphere: In order to tell the story, it is necessary to have a calm and peaceful environment. From the - psychological standpoint, the right environment for story telling is one of curiosity and expectation.

Apart from these suggestions which should be kept in mind, one should consult books on psychology in order to learn the art of storytelling. The educator must critically analyze his own style, language, acting, etc., in order to eliminate the errors he finds.

Story telling is an art. Every teacher, particularly every civics teacher, should know this art, with rich imagination, accurate and wide knowledge of the past and a rich collection of stories to be able to use them when the situation demands.

Lecture Method

Lecture is the oldest procedure of teaching civics through imparting authentic, systematic and effective information about events and trends.

The Objectives

To motivate: While starting the study of a new unit or topic, the teacher may present the outstanding aspect effectively in a lecture. He may refer to some of the significant persons, events and problems and thus arouse the curiosity of the pupils.

To clarify: In the study of a unit, problem or topic, when the pupils are troubled by the same difficulty, lecture can be given to save time. A few minute's lecturing can help to clarify matters and thus save valuable time in the situations calling for review, for new synthesis, for an interpretation, or for the establishment of hitherto unrecognised associations.

To review: By summarising the main points of a unit or topic through lecture, the teacher can very well guide the pupils and indicate some of the important and significant details.

To expand contents: Pupils are interested to know beyond the text-book. They are interested in the teacher's reading, in his travels and in his experiences. This is possible if the teacher manages to give a lecture punctuated with interesting anecdotes, stories, personal experiences and chatty descriptions. Thus, lecture is one of the best ways of presenting additional materials.

As no text-book, however comprehensive it may be, gives the latest and most up-to-date information about these topics lecture, method can prove particularly useful in dealing with units concerning United Nations, Emergence of Asia, Africa, and Latin America, Developing Countries, the Contemporary World and India, International Peace and Cooperation, etc.

The Advantages

Interesting: A well-prepared and well delivered lecture can make civics teaching interesting. The spoken word is frequently far more effective than the printed one. By tones, gestures and facial expressions the teacher can indicate the exact shade of meaning that he wishes to convey, while delivering a lecture. By shifting his position, by impersonating characters, by changing his voice and by using simple devices, he can deliver his message effectively and impart life and blood, colour and vividness to the lifeless and colourless printed material.

Teacher-taught contact: Lecture gives the teacher an opportunity to come into immediate contact with the pupils to see and know whether the pupils are appreciating what he says. He can repeat the message or change the approach and thus manage to carry the pupils along with him.

Listening and Noting: Lecture gives the pupils training in listening and taking rapid notes.

Saving time: Lecture ensures adequate preparation by the teacher. Greater enthusiasm and interest on the part of the teacher is bound to be felt by the pupils as this enthusiasm is somewhat contagious.

Stimulation: Good lectures stimulate brighter pupils. They are prompted to put in more work.

The Limitations

Substitution of the teacher for the pupil: If the teacher is in the habit of giving frequent lectures, he secures valuable experience, but the pupils are deprived of their chance to similar experience. As learning is participating in the learning process, the pupils need the opportunity to talk, to ask questions.

Therefore it is advisable for the teacher to resort to an occasional and informal use of this method.

Reducing opportunity to learn: As readymade 'cooked' material is presented to the pupil the lecture reduces the opportunity for the pupils to learn by doing.

Monotony: Lecture may create a deadening monotony. Only an exceptional teacher can stimulate and keep up the interest of the students continuously.

Suggestions to Make the Lecture Successful

Choosing the occasion: The teacher should choose the occasion for the lecture with great care. Some of the best occasions for the use of this method are the opening of a unit or topic, presentation of additional material, summarising of an extensive topic, clarification of a complex problem, elaboration of a current event. The teacher may give a hint about some topic or unit to be developed in some later lecture so that the pupils, may be led to anticipate the lecture with eagerness.

Synopsis: The teacher should prepare a synopsis of the lecture and give it to the pupils to save the former from pointless digression. It will help the pupils to pay undivided attention to the lecture.

Careful delivery: The teacher must speak clearly and slowly so that the pupils are able to keep pace with him. He should talk to the students rather than lecture to a class. Rise and fall in his voice is necessary to lay emphasis on a point and also to attract the pupils. Frequent natural changes of positions help the speaker to feel at ease and to ensure an equal opportunity to hear to every member of the class.

Humour: Lecture should be enlivened by analogies, comparisons, illustrations and anecdotes bearing upon the topic. Aids such as pictures, films, film strips, slides, diagrams, etc., should be used to make the lecture interesting.

Testing: Lecture should be followed by a written test to measure the success or otherwise of the lecture. If the pupils have learnt well, the lecture is successful, if not, the teacher can revise his methods.

Question-answer Method

This is a popular method of teaching civics. In it the teacher puts the questions to the pupils, while the answers given by the pupils are supplemented and elaborated by him. By asking questions, the relevant experiences in the memory of the students come to the surface while the familiar and known associations help in learning and granting the unfamiliar and the unknown. The pupils readjust the old for acquiring new knowledge. The old and the new get integrated and the process of learning becomes simpler and easier.

To motivate the pupils and create a felt need for learning something new or solve some new problem sometimes, the teacher himself puts questions. Initially questions are asked directly about such past experiences of the pupils which are relevant to the present lesson, in a manner that the present topic appears to the pupils as a problem in whose solution they would be naturally interested. These are generally developmental questions. In the presentation stage both the narrative and developmental questions are used in seeking the solution to the problem developed during the preparation or introduction stage.

The Advantages

Deepening insight: It develops the pupil's insight into the lesson and leads to the understanding and comprehension of the subject matter presented.

Application: In the recapitulation or application stage, questions are asked to find out the grasp of the subject matter or to help the pupils apply the knowledge granted to new situations. Thus, learning in consolidated and insight deepened.

The question-answer is a good method of teaching civics as it ensures active participation of the pupils. It should be supported by visual aids like pictures, charts, films, filmstrips, etc., and devices like dramatization in different forms, sustaining the interest of the pupils.

Observation Method

Direct experiences are more effective in the process of learning. They are retained for a longer period of time. They are rich, full-bodied experiences, purposeful experiences seen, handled, tasted, touched, felt and smelled. They are the unabridged version of life. A trip to the actual site, say a monument, a fort, a temple, an institution, provide the most first-hand experiences. As they are real; children can see them, hear them, ask questions about them and examine them. Such experiences are most edifying and highly conducive to learning. They are a motivating force for further enquiry. Immediate surroundings and community afford many opportunities for observation. Tangible, visible and describable concrete data on cultural, social and political facts and relationships prove invaluable for teaching civics. These lend vitality to the subject-matter of civics. Hence observation method is particularly useful in teaching civics.

Observations under the careful guidance of civics teacher provide ample opportunities for the pupils for asking questions, gathering data and pooling information. Visits to Panchayat and District or Municipal Board in session clarify ideas about local self government.

The Techniques

Field trips: Field trips may be undertaken for securing information, changing attitudes, awakening interests, developing appreciation, promoting ideas and enjoying new experiences. Used to initiate a unit of study ; they may be a part of the core of it or they may give it the finishing touch.

Community surveys: Community surveys foster- comprehensive understanding of community structure and processes in their everyday operation, interaction and complexity. They stimulate insight into community problems and trends influenced by past conditions, present developments and future prospects.

Community service projects: These involve individual activity of an integrated, mental, physical, emotional and spiritual nature resulting in genuine educational value to the pupil as well as significant social value to society.

Observation resources: These vary from community to community. If the teacher is resourceful and class enthusiastic and clever, they can prepare a catalogue of the available resources for proper and detailed study. Proper procedure should be followed for the observation of the resources to achieve maximum benefit for the pupils.

Conversational Method

In it the teacher puts the question to the pupils while the answers given by the pupils lead to the development of the lesson to be presented. The teacher supplements and elaborates the answers of the pupils from time to time. By asking questions, the relevant past experiences come to the fore and the familiar and known associations help in learning and grasping the unfamiliar and unknown. For acquiring the new knowledge, the pupils readjust the old and the new and the process of learning civics gets simplified.

Sometimes, the teacher puts questions to the pupils to motivate them and create a felt need for the solution of a problem: Initially, questions are asked directly about past experiences of the pupils relevant to the present lesson, in a fashion that the present lesson appears to them as a problem in whose solution they would be naturally interested. These are generally developmental questions. Both the narrative and developmental questions are used in seeking the solution to the problem developed during the preparation stage. They develop pupils' insight into the lesson and lead to the learning of the subject-matter presented. Learning is consolidated and insight deepened in the application stage when questions are asked to help pupils apply the knowledge gained to new situations.

The Advantages

The Conversational method or Question-Answer method is quite a good method of teaching civics. It should be supported by visual aids like pictures, charts, models, films, filmstrips and devices like dramatization in different forms. This makes learning of civics an interesting experience for the pupils.

Note-dictation

Some teachers use note-dictation as one of the methods of teaching civics for the following reasons

Absence of suitable text-books: The absence of suitable text-books is one of the reasons for the use of this method by most of civics teachers. Some topics are magnified beyond proportion in text-books because they have some individual appeal for the author, while others receive scanty treatment. The language of the text-books is tough as they are written by university and college teachers who neither have experience of teaching youngsters nor are teachers conversant with their psychological needs. This makes the reading material tough and beyond the comprehension of average students. Teachers start dictating notes to get speedy results.

Pressure of work: A civics teacher is often overburdened with work. Expected to take at least thirty-three periods a week, he does not get enough time for thorough preparation. He is generally allotted some period towards the fag-end of the day when most of the pupils are already tired due to strenuous work put in the preceding periods. In such exacting subjects as Mathematics, English, etc., the teacher starts dictating notes to avoid the distraction of attention on the part of students due to exhaustion, and to keep them engaged.

Shortage of time: The curriculum in civics is overcrowded. To finish the course in time, the Civics teacher looks for a short-cut-dictation of notes.

External examination: Teachers dictate notes of important and expected questions to get good results in external examination.

Inadequate power of expression: Civics teachers lacking the power of expression can neither narrate nor lecture well. They resort to note-dictation and are saved the trouble of making preparation for narration or lecture.

Practices in Vogue

Detailed notes on important topics: Some teachers prefer to give detailed notes on important topics only, viz., on topics such as international peace and cooperation, local self government, etc. The notes are given, after the teacher has already discussed the topics in the class.

In the form of substance: After explaining the topic in detail some teachers give notes in the form of substance on the black-board. They, sometimes, also require the pupils to prepare the lesson in advance at home. Pupils are asked to copy the substance from the black-board.

Question answer form: Some teachers prefer to give notes in the question-answer form selecting important and expected questions and dictating their answers.

Limitations

1. Note dictation is a malady eating into the vitals of civics teaching. The dictated notes do not give any training in the use of critical powers, which is one of the important aims of teaching civics. A pupil takes the matter dictated by the teacher as gospel truth and crams it without testing the relevance of the material.
2. This method is based on the mistaken notion that instruction is a process of memorisation and civics teaching is synonymous with the memorisation of facts communicated by the teacher.
3. Pupils start disregarding the text-books. They do not develop the habit of consulting reference books. They fail to develop proper insight into the subject.

While teaching civics, it is essential to make the pupils think and express, consult all possible works on the subject and prepare their own notes.

Discussion Method

Discussion is one of the most valuable methods of teaching civics. It is said that "Two heads are better than one" but, when a number of heads combine to solve a problem, wonderful results are achieved.

A problem, an issue, a situation about which there is a difference of opinion, is most suitable for discussion method of teaching civics. Ideas are initiated, opinions exchanged, accompanied by a search for its factual basis. Speech is free and responsible. Values are created, the participants are engaged in a process of competitive cooperation. Agreement is the declared purpose of discussion which is, an ordered process of collective decision making. If agreement is not reached, discussion has the value of clarifying and sharpening the nature of agreement.

Objectives

As a method of teaching civics, discussion may be used for the following purposes:

1. To lay plans for new work ;
2. To make decisions concerning future action ;
3. To share information ;
4. To obtain and gain respect for various points of view ;
5. To clarify ideas ;
6. To inspire interest ; and
7. To evaluate progress.

Steps Involved in the Discussion Method

In the case of Problems

(i) Locating and defining problems of common interest and significance ;

(ii) Working together to find ways of solving the problems ;

(iii) Allocating responsibilities for the solutions suggested ; and

(iv) Evaluating the effectiveness of the suggested solutions and their implementations.

In the case of plans for projects and programmes:

(i) Deciding on the programme and the particulars such as date, time and place.

(ii) Enumerating the jobs to be done in organising the programme;

(iii) Allocating duties to the members of the group ; and

(iv) Evaluating the results.

Forms of Discussion

Discussion may be classified as a classroom discussion, a debate, a symposium, a panel discussion or brain storming, etc.

Debate

It is a programme in which two or more students present arguments holding contradictory opinions on a particular problem. They are given an opportunity to rebut the opposite side. The rest of the class is encouraged to ask questions from the debaters or engage in a brief discussion with them. A debate has a moderator. In order to get significant results, the teacher should work both with the debaters and the class. Some useful topics for debate in Civics Teaching may be :

1. Democracy is the best form of government.
2. For forms of government let fools contest, that which is governed least is best.
3. Democracy in India is more formal than real.
4. Preventive detention of citizens by the government deprives them of their fundamental rights.
5. In a backward democracy, fundamental rights are of no use, etc.

Symposium

In symposium the participants present their views to the audience about various aspects of a selected problem or topic through speeches or paper reading. In the words of Struck, "We think of a symposium as a group of comments, either spoken or written, which portray contrasting or at least different points of view." The chief objective of the symposium is to clarify thought upon controversial questions.

The general audience listens to the discussions. Each person forms his own conclusions concerning the validity or value of the points of view presented. The ideal number of pupil participants in a symposium is four or five.

Symposia may be arranged on such topics as :

1. Local self Government
2. Panchayat as village government
3. Gandhi and his thoughts
4. Rights and Duties of a citizen
5. Democracy as the best form of government.
6. Declaration of assets and liabilities of the Ministers, etc.

Panel discussion

It is a discussion among a selected group of four to six persons, large enough for variety and small enough for purposeful deliberations. The participants are usually eminent in their fields, they present various points of view before an audience which joins in the discussion subsequently. The purpose of panel discussion is to get important facts from different angles, to stimulate thinking and lay a basis for wide participation. No speeches are made by the members or by the leader. Only informal conversations take place.

Kinds of panel discussions

In a panel discussion, one can follow either the rotation system where each member expresses his opinion in turn or the members may speak briefly as the thought comes to them one after the other.

The Advantages

The panel discussion provides a natural setting in which people have the opportunity to ask questions, to evaluate replies and to contribute constructively.

Topics for panel discussions

1. The role of Panchayats in rural development
2. Democracy can no longer solve the problems of underdeveloped countries.
3. "The President represents the nation but does not rule the nation. He is the symbol of the nation."
4. "An active king, whose opinions were a matter of public concern, is unthinkable within the framework of our (England's) constitution"-Laski.
5. "The Parliamentary system produces a stronger government for (a) members of the Executive and Legislatures are overlapping and (b) the heads of the government control the legislature"- K.M. Munshi, etc., etc.

Brain Storming

In this method of discussion the brains of the participants are stimulated to create a storm of ideas and provide suggestions regarding the topic without any deliberation to find whether or not they are meaningful and purposeful. The principle behind this method is that when the brain is let go thus without social inhibitions, it would be able to give expression to some of the most useful and practical suggestions. "Students could do a lot to strengthen the cooperative movement" is quite a good topic for brain storming.

The Procedure

Planning: Discussion method can produce the desired results only if the teacher and student representatives do considerable planning. It requires a well-directed procedure.

Preparation: For thorough preparation for the discussion, the teacher should read wide and deep enough purposefully and critically and prepare the material conscientiously. Points to be discussed should be arranged logically, written on the chalk board for guidance. The problem to be discussed should be a felt problem.

Conduct of discussion: While conducting the discussion, the teacher should see that it is disciplined. The arrangement of seats should ensure face-to-face talk. As the strength of the discussion is obtained from the information and viewpoint of all members of the group, all contribute to its progress. It is a thinking together process which should not be dominated by one or more members of the group. The teacher must see that every member of the group participates. He should encourage sincere questions and comments. The discussion must be geared to the realization of specific objectives and development of proper skills and methods.

A relaxed and informal climate: It is essential to obtain desirable results to be achieved. The discussion should be truly a cooperative experience, not a competitive quarrel. Discouraging attack upon persons the teacher should seek to bring the participants to focus their comments on the proposition not the person. A discussion should be objective-oriented. Questions should be skilful and direction sound. A happy rapport should be established between the teacher and the taught.

Evaluation: Discussion must conclude in certain achievements such as expanding information or lessening or removing prejudices, changing attitudes or ideals, increasing the range of his interest, altering his ideas concerning national and international policies, or causing him to become a more active citizen.

The Advantages

Useful both for the juniors and seniors: On the lower level, children learn to take turns, listen attentively, act cooperatively, speak distinctly, stand and sit correctly, respect the ideas of others, share interests, ask pertinent questions, utilize simple information and comprehend the problem before the group. On the upper level, they plan and discuss problems with the entire group and in smaller units. A group learns together and presents important information, makes suggestions, shares responsibility, comprehends the topic, evaluates the findings and summarises results.

Clarification and sharpening of the issues: As new ground is discovered both for agreement and disagreement old ideas and values may be replaced by new ones.

Crystallisation of thinking and identification of concepts: Thus, their knowledge of civics becomes clear.

Knowing and understanding: The difference in perspective need not result in disaster.

Discovering what he did not know: What he has overlooked and wherein he is mistaken. He may find out what he knows and with what surety he knows it.

Giving knowledge a round trip: Discussion is not a one way affair of the teacher. It engenders more reflection than the question and answer recitation. Of all the methods of teaching social studies, it is farthest from rote learning. In place of cajolary, threat, coercion or propaganda, it employs reasonable persuasion.

Representing a type of intellectual team-work: Resting on the philosophy and principle that the pooled knowledge, ideas and feelings of several persons have greater merit than those of a single individual, discussion is valuable as a team work.

Tolerance: Discussion engenders toleration for views which are at variance from those one holds.

Self-evaluation: Discussion activates thinking along the lines of self-evaluation helpful in establishing an attitude of looking forward to progress and growth.

Discovery of talents: Discussion can help the teacher in discovering students who have a potential for becoming genuine leaders.

4
Teaching Methods—II

Assignment Method

This method is advocated for the teaching of civics in higher classes. In it the whole of the syllabus is split into significant topics, each topic is sub-divided into assignments. The pupils are required to prepare the assignments in writing as written assignments help in organisation of knowledge, assimilation of facts and better preparation for examinations.

Types of assignments

Preparatory assignments: These assignments are meant for the purpose of circulation. The pupils are prepared for the work which is to follow on the next day. This pilot work enables the teacher to lead the class with ease and understanding.

Study assignments: Study assignment can be problem solving assignments, assignments on making and handling tools, assignments on picture reading, assignments for the preparation of a topic in the light of references provided.

Revisional assignments: These assignments are given for (a) providing drill to the work done by the students, and (b) for checking their retention and reproduction of facts, incidents, etc,. of the topic and (c) for checking the understanding of the topic. They are worked out in advance according to the specific objectives of the subject-matter being tested.

Remedial assignments: Devised in the light of pupil's reactions to the three types of assignments mentioned above, the purpose of these assignments is to remove weak points and clear misunderstandings.

Steps in an assignment lesson

Preparation: In this step, efforts are made for developing the pupil's interest in writing, the assignment. Broad heads are outlined under which the assignment is to be written. The necessary information are given including the reference, etc., which would help the pupils in working out the assignment. This work should be completed in one period.

Writing: The pupils may write the assignment at home. Writing in the class under the supervision of the teacher, they should be allowed the facilities to consult books and ask questions whenever necessary. This may take more than one class period.

Selection of pairs for mutual corrections: The pupils are given a list of the types of probable errors which may occur in writing civics assignments to help them in correction work. Common errors may be : omission of vital facts, wrong statement of facts, statement of irrelevant facts, failure to bring out causal relationships, etc. The pupils are to point out all these.

Correction by pupils: The pupils are asked to correct their assignments at home.

Correction of sample assignment scripts by the teacher.

Preparation of common list of errors.

Discussion of the list in a correction class: The common errors committed by the pupils are discussed in a correction class to check their recurrence.

The Advantages

Knowledge of interests: It enables the teacher to know the interests of his pupils. He discovers the specific abilities of the individual pupil to be developed and used for their own good.

Foreseeing difficulties: The teacher foresees the difficulties which the students may have to face in the learning of the topic. He guides the pupils by putting thought-provoking questions in his assignments.

The questions and guidance to study a topic prepares the pupils to face the difficulties boldly.

Suitable for pupils of different ability levels: Gifted, average and slow.

Project Method

The most concrete of all types of activity methods, Project Method provides learning experiences suited to individual differences.

Meaning: Project is an activity willingly undertaken by the pupils for the solution of a felt problem. It leads to learning as prescribed in the curriculum. It is a concrete activity directed towards the learning of a significant skill or process. It can be taken to include any activity like dramatics, pageants, making models, drawing maps and charts, collecting pictures, preparing scrap books, going on historical tours and exhibitions, preparation of civics wall newspaper, organisation of debates, etc.

Basic principles

Activity: The project should involve mental or motor activity.

Purpose: It should be purposeful; a felt need of the pupils.

Experiences: It should provide varied type of experiences to the pupils such as manipulative, concrete, mental, etc,

Reality: It should provide real experiences.

Freedom: The pupils should be free to undertake the different activities connected with the project.

Utility: The project should be useful.

Steps in a Project

Providing a situation: In a suitable situation the pupils feel a spontaneous craving for carrying out a useful activity. The teacher discovers the interests, needs, tastes and aptitudes of the pupils through conversation, discussion, exhibition of pictures, models, etc.

Telling a story or taking the pupils out on a field trip initiates them to the world of projects. Exposed to so many situations they are in a position to determine the selection of the project. Opportunities should be given to express their own ideas and to have discussions among themselves, as well as with the teacher. The situations or problems to provide to the pupils, should preferably be social to provide better social training.

Choosing and purposing: One of the important duties of the teacher is to guide the pupils to choose a good project. To quote Dr. Kilpatrik "The part of the pupil and part of the teacher in most of the school work depends largely on who does the purposing. It is practically the whole thing." However the most important thing about a project is its purposing part. To get quick and good results, the teacher may have however the temptation of making the choice of the project himself. This way violates the most important principle of the method, as the final selection of the project should be made by the pupils. Self-choice and self-imposition enable the pupils to work whole-heartedly and energetically. They are stimulated to better planning, thorough execution and successful completion of the project. The teachers guidance to pupil-effort should in no way hinder the development of the pupils. The final choice of the project must be made by the pupils. The project "must enlist the whole-hearted enlistment of the student."

The teacher has to see that the projects chosen satisfy a real felt need of the children and also have educative potentialities. He should expose the pros and cons of the project, let the children reconsider their decision. He should scrupulously resist the temptation of imposing his own ideas on the pupils as they seldom take interest in an activity thrust upon them.

After the choice of the project the pupils may write in their note-book the reasons for their choice which will help them to collect their ideas regarding the choice.

Planning: Planning of the project should be done by the pupils under the guidance of the teacher. The teacher should draw the attention of the pupils to the necessity of the good plan. Discussion should be held in which the pupils and the teacher should be free to express opinions and give suggestions. After taking stock of the resources and limitations of various plans, a plan is drawn up. It requires time and consideration before a really good plan can be made. The whole plan should be written down by the pupils in their notebooks.

The teacher should prepare two or three possible plans in his own mind so as to be ready with replies and all kinds of help to the pupils.

Execution: When the plan of the project is ready, pupils should be encouraged to start work on it. They should distribute the various parts among themselves according to individual interests and capacities. The teacher should see that every pupil is assigned some work and contributes something towards the successful completion of the project. He should not give too much help to speed up the work.

Evaluation: Through evaluation or appraisal of the work pupils find out their shortcomings and good points. After the execution step, the pupils review their work to ensure that nothing has been omitted and that the work has been carried out in accordance with the plan laid down. The mistakes committed are noted to serve as eye-openers for the future. Useful experiences and successes are reviewed to serve as good examples. The pupils critically appraise their work.

Recording: As impressions left unrecorded are likely to be wiped away from memory pupils should be encouraged to maintain a complete record of all activities in the project book connected with the project ; the discussions held, proposals advanced and accepted, duties assigned, books and journals consulted, information sought for, work undertaken, difficulties felt and experiences gained and short and long-term gains obtained. Self-appraisal, along with important guidelines and future references, should be noted down. Well prepared project books may be awarded prizes.

Examples of Projects

1. Story of Transportation through the Ages
2. The Indian Renaissance
3. The Big World, etc.
4. Our Town
5. Nationalist Movement in India
6. Achievement of Independence
7. The Socialist Movement
8. UNO and Its Achievements.

The Advantages

Conforming psychological laws of learning: Project method provides the most natural conditions of learning. Pupil remembers the principles learnt for a longer time.

Freedom: Project method is a method of self-direction. The pupil learns to improvise, to invent, to experiment, to find knowledge in all ways possible, to translate the knowledge into action until the need is met developing the creative mind.

Maturation: The project method provides the sort of learning material that suits a particular stage of mental development. While the more mature pupils are likely to go for the abstract and difficult features of the task in hand, the simple elements will be left to the others.

Social benefits: As separate groups take responsibility for making their own contributions which are subsequently pooled and become the class effort, the method results in social benefits.

Training for social adjustment: Project method aims at developing in the pupils the capacity to adapt themselves to their environment, to make use of whatever is available and to meet a situation resourcefully.

Saves from insincerity and superficiality: In carrying out their purpose the pupils learn and do because they understand the value of what they learn and do.

Training for a democratic way of life: Project method encourages children to co-operate, to think and act together for a common goal. Teaching students to be responsible, it gives them freedom within the framework of co-operative democracy.

Learning through practical problems: Project method encourages pupils to achieve a deeper insight into principles through actually seeing them in operation.

Growth. Both the student and the teacher grow through this method Stimulated and encouraged in his exploration of many materials the student ultimately approaches other areas of learning in a similar manner. The teacher grows in his understanding of a child's creative development.

Evaluation: An intrinsic standard of evaluation is set up in project method. The pupils learn to evaluate their own work. This self evaluation shows the mistakes and *Holistic satisfaction* makes for rapid progress and true learning.

Holistic satisfaction: The pupil gets the satisfaction of completing the whole of task. Organised according to the project method, work is divided into definite tasks to be completed by the child who sees before him a definite unit of work and gains the pleasure of a completed task. By dividing work into a series of projects, the child can finish it in a reasonable time and then have something definite to show for his work. While making learning more interesting, project makes it more effective. Pupils get joy and pride in the finished product of their labours.

The Limitations

1. The practical difficulties of covering a syllabus rule out the project method as the basis of teaching in most schools. Children taught bv the project method often show astonishing knowledge of

details in odd things revealing depths of real ignorance outside the projects.

2. At a later stage of education, it is not so easy to formulate projects having a satisfactory degree of width and comprehensiveness.

3. There is grew difficulty in ensuring any kind of systematic progress in instruction.

4. Very highly qualified teachers are required for success in this method. These teachers should be zealous and well-prepared.

Problem Method

The problem-solving approach to learning in civics is one of training children in the technique of discovery. More than learning the formalized procedures for the solution of problems it is more than analytical thinking that proceeds a step at a time. Development of effectiveness in intuitive thinking, it is learning to utilise adequate modes of thought. It is learning that art of predictive reasoning, of manipulating knowledge to make it fit new tasks. It is developing a style of problem solving that will serve for most of the difficulties in life. By generalising what they have learned about the solving of intellectual problems in civics, children solve their problems of social living efficiently and effectively.

In contrast to the project method, in problem method emphasis is laid on the mental solution reached rather than on a practical accomplishment. The major purpose of the problem method is to afford training for the pupil and reforming their opinion and future attitudes.

Steps in problem method

1. Discovering, considering, discussing, selecting and starting the specific problem or question.
2. Collecting, organising, comparing and judging significant information in the light of the defined problem.

3. Exploring the problem and framing some possible solutions.
4. Drawing preliminary conclusions for further exploration and study.
5. Evaluating findings and establishing a conclusion.
6. Considering the summarization with the possibility of further study.

Problem Selection

Intellectually challenging: The problem should stimulate critical thinking, evoke a desire to seek cause and effect relationships, and to discover reasons as well as information. It should open up opportunities for formulating and testing generalisations.

Touching the lives of majority of the children: Within the realm of their past experiences the problems should have an impact upon the children.

Centering on a basic human activity: Illuminating man's effort to meet his basic human activities the problem should shed light on the role of basic human activities in community life.

Practical problem: To assure meaningful development of the problem, there should be an adequate number of opportunities available in the community. The range of instructional resources should be sufficient to meet the varying duties of children.

New and expanding interests: The problem should lead to new and expanding interests among the pupils not only in the development of the problem itself but also in a variety of the side interests it stimulates.

The Advantages

Sequence of learning: Experiences undertaken to solve problems and answer questions result in a sequence of learnings. To solve a specific problem the facts and information have to be marshalled leading to concepts, undertakings, attitudes and skills, which pave the way for generalisations for civics which help achieve elementary school objectives.

Realistic method: Problem-solving is a realistic method for presenting the experience that will face the pupil throughout his career. It gives him a chance to think, to judge, to evaluate, to compare and select what is best. He is challenged to bring to bear all his information and experience in such a problem, arousing his interest and awakening his curiosity as to how it can be done.

Pupil's objective: The problem furnishes an objective of the pupil because he can easily see its significance and the importance of securing its solution.

Logical way of thinking: This method points out a logical way of thinking to the pupils. They can see the necessity and sequence of following each step properly.

Evaluation and reorganisation: The pupils learn to track down information quickly and efficiently, to evaluate, to think, to deduce the truth from different viewpoints, to tell what is real and what is propaganda, to organise ideas and draw conclusions.

Adjustment: The problem can be adjusted to groups and to individuals to promote the proper amount of adaptation without sacrificing the social values that arise from co-operative understanding.

Initiative and responsibility: The problem tends to develop initiative and responsibility. The process is not a task which is assigned, but an inevitable requirement of the solution.

Open-mindedness and tolerance: These traits develop because the pupils see many sides to a problem and listen to many points of view. Their horizon of thinking is widened. They learn to think critically and independently and to struggle for solutions to selected problems.

Proper relationship: Good and harmonious relations are established and promoted between teacher and pupil. The pupil feels free from arbitrarily imposed tasks of the teacher and learns to appreciate the guidance of the teacher. Thus, a foundation is laid for good and happy relations between teacher and taught leading to the success of the teaching-learning process.

Adjustment to needs: In a small unit or a long term assignment the problem can be adjusted according to the needs.

The Limitations

Problem Method too has certain limitations

Monotony: According to Maurice P Moffatt this method will become monotonous if used too frequently. Therefore, it can not be used as the sole method.

Social pertinence: The problem method is in danger of implying a social pertinence and value that it very seldom achieves.

Over estimation: Problem solving in the classroom means solution of simple problems, just to give training to the pupils. But the solution of simple problems may easily lead the pupil to think that he has acquired a technique applicable to complex social problems as well as to classroom exercises.

Too advanced: Edger Bruce Wesley believes that the problem method may lead to the selection of trivial and untimely topics, and in some instances to those that generate more feeling and emotion than thought. This may be avoided if the teacher is very cautious in selecting the problems. As Wesley writes, 'The problem method may become a seminar method that is too advanced for the pupils."

Intellectual change to the pupils: In problem method the problems are largely intellectual in their nature, constant use of which may lead to too little attention to activities.

Socialised Recitation Method

Socialised Recitation method can be used in civics for the introduction of a topic and for studying a problem. It eliminates the limitations of traditional and formal classroom teaching. Group thinking is developed, the classroom becomes a unit of dynamic group life ; the pupils have a sense of freedom as no one is repressed. He develops reflective thinking, supplements previous knowledge, has creative expression, develops desirable social attitudes by practicing in a large variety of socialised situations, and having opportunities for practice in the techniques of cooperative thinking.

Techniques of socialised recitation method: (1) Seminar, (2) Workshop, (3) Symposium (4) Panel discussion (5) Brains Trust.

Socialised Recitation

Committee meeting: It can be a sort of committee meeting in which the members decide on an agenda, express their ideas freely, share their information willingly and eventually come to some conclusion about an issue or a problem.

Class discussion: The whole class may carry on the discussion with teacher as the discussion leader.

Under a chairman: The class elects a chairman to guide the discussion and discussion takes the form of socialised recitation.

Parliament: The class may be organised as a parliamentary group with a president, a vice-president and other special office bearers.

Procedure involved in the method: 1. Planning, 2. Conducting, 3. Reporting, 4. Evaluating.

The Advantages

Training for participation in social environment: It provides with opportunities for participation to the pupils with ease and freedom in conversation, the readiness to mix in friendly groups and the ability to work in co-operation for the interest of the class as a whole.

Ensures increased learning: The democratic procedure in determining classroom activities results in increased learning.

Development of leadership qualities: Opportunities are provided to the pupils for participation in a number of socialised situations and get a chance for development of leadership traits.

Democracy in action: It develops a faith in the ability of pupils to work cooperatively in the solution of problems. The combined intelligence of all members of this group proves greater than the sum of their separate insights. Co-operative thinking produces better decisions than those rendered by individuals.

Practice in correct parliamentary procedure

The Limitations

1. Socialised recitation is time-consuming, permits a few pupils to dominate the discussion, produces monotony, is difficult to organise and manage and permits wandering from the topic.
2. Arthur C. Bining and David H. Bining write, "One great danger in the use of the method resides in the likelihood that the lesson will be socialised in name only. In other words, we shall have the form but not the substance... the procedure may become mechanical and pupils respond not through any social urge but through habit or desire to please the teacher. Under such procedure, the method has less value than the old type recitation."
3. Socialised recitation is wasteful of time. It is not conducive to an adequate mastery of the subject-matter of social studies.

Suggestions to make Recitation effective

1. It should centre round a topic which is important from the pupil's point of view.
2. The teacher should prepare everything.
3. During the period of socialised recitation, a friendly atmosphere must prevail.

4. The teacher should have good control.

5. It should never be used to promote the spread of prejudice.

Source Method

Objectives

1. To develop critical thinking by using the sources and weighing the evidence.

2. To form their own independent judgement through a critical analysis of sources.

3. To develop elementary skills of collecting data, sifting the relevant data, organising them and interpreting them.

4. To create proper atmosphere so as to make the people and events of bygone times more real.

5. To stimulate the imagination of the students for reconstructing the past.

6. To develop and promote interest in the study of social studies in the right perspective.

Different Stages

Lower stage: Dr. Keatings has pointed out that original sources can be used for creating atmosphere in the lower forms. Such a use of the sources does not necessitate any great exposition.

Secondary stage: The pupils should be encouraged to collect, examine and correlate the facts and even to compare and rationalise different conflicting accounts of characters. The exercise, to begin with, should be fairly simple and graded in difficulty.

Use of sources at various steps of the lesson

Pre-lesson use of sources: Sources can be used to motivate the pupils for a particular lesson.

Mid-lesson use of sources: The use of sources can be made for developing the lesson.

Post-lesson use of sources: Sources can be used by the teacher after he finishes the lesson. Interesting and useful extracts from the original or secondary sources may be given to the students and they may be asked to write answers to some questions on their basis.

The Advantages

1. It develops a sense of vividness and reality.
2. It can satisfy the curiosity among children on the question- "how do we know this?"
3. The original sources serve as an effective means for creating a right type of atmosphere.
4. The use of sources provides certain useful mental exercises such as right thinking and imagination, comparing and analysing, drawing inferences, self-expression and discussion.
5. The original sources can be used to illustrate more important points in support of an oral lesson or to supplement the one-sided picture of historical, political, economic and social accounts.
6. The method initiates the pupils in research.
7. Though the method is most suitable for the pupils of higher classes, it can be used with advantage by the pupils of primary classes also.

The Limitations

1. It is not always possible for the teacher of schools to have easy access to original sources.
2. Use of sources is not easy for the teachers.
3. The method is too complex and technical.

4. The sources available are in many languages and scripts covering a period of more than three thousand years.

5. There is also the difficult problem of sifting the suitable evidences from a multiplicity of sources.

Unit Method

This method is of foreign origin quite popular in the United States of America. Gestalt's psychological theories have played a vital role in its development. It is proposed to present the subject matter for teaching as a whole. In the words of Henry C. Morrison: "Unit is a comprehensive and significant aspect of the environment, of an organised science and an art. This is intended to make the teaching easy and convenient. For the convenience of teaching, a subject matter is divided into certain units".

Steps of Unit

Morrison has laid down the following five steps of a unit: -

Exploration: The students are prepared for a new unit. An attempt is made to explore their past knowledge.

Presentation: Through lecture and narration the teacher tries to present an outline of the unit to be presented before the students.

Assimilation: The students try to own and acquire the information that is provided to them.

Recording: The students try to organise the information that they have assimilated.

Recitation: The students try to express in form of a lecture or action that they have acquired.

The Merits

1. It creates interests in the pupils for the subject.

2. It is based on the idea of giving whole knowledge to the pupils and tries to remove the shyness of the pupils.

3. The pupils are taught to draw up plans of action, which is helpful for their future life.

4. It is based on individual differences and develops the habit of self-study.

5. The pupils are taught the lesson of carrying out their duties sincerely and shouldering the responsibilities properly.

6. It develops the qualities of sympathy, love, tolerance, leadership, discipline, etc.

The Limitations

1. It is not useful for all subjects.

2. It does not train the students in the art of appreciation.

3. It is a very expensive method consuming a lot of time.

4. It lays stress on imparting knowledge of the whole to the students, so either the pupils acquire a whole knowledge or do not acquire any knowledge at all.

5. It may degenerate into a mechanical method.

Laboratory Method

Civics is a social science. So some scholars are of the view that the teaching of Civics should be conducted in a laboratory, equipped with materials, connected with the subject matter of Civics. The pupils should be encouraged to acquire knowledge independently. As soon as pupils enter the laboratory they should think that they are the future citizens of India.

Equipment of Laboratory

1. A room with space for seating of 30 to 40 boys

2. A good number of chairs and desks.

3. Blackboard preferably painted green.

4. Arrangement for models, pictures, maps, sketches, charts, lists and such other things.
5. Bulletin board
6. Almirahs and book-shelves.
7. Books that are lodged should deal with Civics.
8. Films and slides.
9. Radio and, a television set. In poor countries television shall be extremely expensive.
10. Magazines, Dictionaries, Encyclopaedias, etc.
11. Other teaching aids.

Role of the teacher: The teacher determines the whole programme. He draws up the entire outline of the work. He gives an idea of the programme to the pupils with the help of available sources. He determines the time, during which the work is to be completed. The pupils have to finish the work within that prescribed period. If a pupil finishes the work beforehand, then he is allotted some other work.

There is a progress report for every student in which are entered details of the work done by him.

Though this method is expensive, but it helps the students to take to independent teaching. Individuality and activity are the essentials of this method of teaching.

Dramatic Method

Based on the theory of- 'Play', attempt is made to get the subject matter enacted or dramatised with the help of the students who take interest in dramatising the subject-matter.

The working of the Parliament or Zila Parishads may be dramatised with the help of the students.

The Merits

1. It brings about a development of the mental faculties.
2. Interest is created in the students about the subject that has to be taught.
3. The subject-matter of Civics is made interesting and intelligible.
4. It creates a sense of self-confidence and self-importance.
5. It leads to development of social and moral qualities. Pupils try to liveup to the ideals of the great men whose role they play.

The Requirements

1. The teacher should be well aware of the techniques of drama. He should also know the art of writing dialogues.
2. He should have the capacity to select the dramatic material.
3. He should be acquainted with the qualities of simplicity and authenticity that are the requisites of dramatic procedure.
4. He should have the capacity to mould his personality accordingly, as and when required.

QUESTIONS

1. Narrate briefly the various methods which can be adopted for the teaching of civics in the primary classes. Which one of these do you like the most and why?
2. Narrate briefly the various methods which can be adopted for the teaching of civics in the, secondary classes. Which one of these do you like the most and why?
3. Discuss in detail the main characteristics of the Lecture Method of teaching civics. What are the advantages and disadvantages of this method?

4. Discuss the advantages of story method of teaching civics.
5. 'Observation Method is one of the best methods of teaching civics'. How will you ensure the success of this method?
6. Discuss with illustrations. How you would use the following methods in teaching civics
   (a) Conversational Method
   (b) Project Method
   (c) Discussion Method
   (d) Assignment Method, and
   (e) Note-Dictation.
7. What do you know about Discussion Method of teaching civics? What precautions will you bear in mind to make discussion useful and interesting? Discuss the advantages of this in detail.
8. Describe fully, under the following headings in a 'Project' in civics which you would like to carry out
   (a) Age of children
   (b) Preliminary discussion
   (c) The teacher's preparation
   (d) The part played by children
   (e) The development of the project
   (f) The achievement hoped for and gained.
9. What is meant by Problem Solving? Describe the various steps in teaching civics through problem solving. What considerations are you going to bear in mind in making a choice of suitable problems for solution?
10. How would you use any one of the following methods in senior classes for increasing effective participation by your pupils?
    (a) Source Method
    (b) Project Method.

In your answer you may: (a) identify different activities you would design ; (b) give your plan for employing these activities in your teaching, or (c) explain the procedure to assess the learning outcomes.

11. In the light of your knowledge of the Discussion Method of teaching civics how will you discuss the following statement with the students of X class? "The solution of the problem of disarmament cannot be found within the problem itself ; but outside it, as the problem is not one of disarmament as such but rather the organisation of the world community."

12. How will you use socialised recitation as one of the methods of teaching civics?

5
Teaching Techniques

Devices and Maxims

In the process of teaching civics, the teacher has to resort to the use of certain *techniques, devices* and *maxims* to facilitate and promote learning.

Techniques: A technique means a method of performance, manipulation, everything concerned with the mechanical part of an artistic performance. "A time-honoured method of imparting knowledge to pupils is connected with oral teaching." Important techniques of teaching civics are explanation, narration and description.

Devices: Devices are "certain external forms or modes which the instruction may from time to time assume." Devised or designed these different modes of presentation are *questioning-answering, illustration, home work, the use of library, and text-books, notes-assignments, - supervised* study, etc. These devices or modes of presentation and teaching are used to foster the development of knowledge and attitudes among pupils.

Maxims: The maxims are general principles serving as rules or guides. Well-known maxims of methodical procedure useful to the teacher, are proceeding from the known to the unknown, simple to the complex, indefinite to the definite, concrete to the abstract, particular to the general, psychological to logical, empirical to rational, etc.

The Techniques

Techniques of civics teaching do not have their individual

capacity. They are a part and parcel of the method of teaching. They are ways of teaching Civics to the students at different stages. An additional help to the methods of teaching, they are employed for making the teaching more effective and interesting. To quote Prof. M.P Moffat, 'All techniques should be in line with the democratic process and relate to the goals desired in the study of the topic. Techniques are employed for getting the learning under way with guidance from the teacher. They should be selected as a means of serving the best purpose of a particular line with the resultant growth for the individual."

(1) Question-answer technique

(2) Illustration

(3) Home Work

(4) Notes

(5) Assignment

(6) Supervised Study

Question-answer Technique

Questions have a very important place in the teaching of Civics. By questioning, the students may be kept attentive and active. The teacher can also test if he has succeeded in imparting the knowledge to the students.

It can also be safely tested whether the students have actually acquired the knowledge of the subject taught.

The Utility

Questioning technique or the Question-answer technique can bring about the following achievements:

Awakening interest and curiosity of the students.

Encouraging the students to finish their work, within a prescribed period of time.

Developing the various mental powers of the students, namely : reasoning, thinking, imagination, etc.

Encouraging the students to take to research and discovery of new things.

Helping the students to present their various problems so that their solution may be brought about.

Helping in testing the knowledge of the students.

Classification of the questions

Questions may be of various types such as the following

(i) Questions that awaken and develop memory

(ii) Reasoning questions

(iii) Organising questions

(iv) Informative questions

(v) Evaluating questions

(vi) Comparative questions

(vii) Analytic questions

(viii) Thought-provoking questions

(ix) Interpretative questions

(x) Judicative questions.

Required Abilities of Educator

The difficulty of this technique lies in asking of the appropriate questions. Though even the biggest fool can ask an unanswerable question, the question asked in the classroom must have some educative value. Asking such questions is no less than an art. This art, which is one aspect of the technique, is acquired through continuous practice. What is really required is complete awareness of the purpose of asking a particular question. The educator himself must possess the following abilities in order to phrase his questions skillfully:-

Accurate and comprehensive knowledge of the subject: In order to ask appropriate questions, the educator must have comprehensive knowledge of the subject, as otherwise the questions are likely to be useless. It is only this knowledge which tells the educator the questions he must ask in order to teach something.

Ability to analyse the subject: The teacher's ability in asking questions depends upon his ability to analyse the subject matter and to locate the areas of difficulty inherent in it.

Knowledge of the educand: Before embarking on questions, the educator must have knowledge of the educand's psychology so that the questions may conform to the latter's mental level, abilities and motivation.

Experience: Much of the facility, variety and accuracy of the questions depend upon the educator's experience.

Mental ability and decisiveness: In order to ask the right questions, the educator himself must have mental ability and the power to arrive at a decision quickly.

Power of expression: Linguistic ability is essential in asking questions. The educator must also have experience in modulating his voice properly.

Reasons for Asking

The various reasons for asking questions are the following :

Motivation: Through questions motivation is created in the educand by arousing his curiosity, focusing his attention and awakening his interest.

Knowledge relating to the educand: The object of many questions is to find out the educand's problems, attitudes, aptitudes, knowledge, etc. Hence, one of the objectives of asking such questions is to provide the teacher with adequate knowledge concerning the educand.

Relating to old knowledge: Another reason for asking questions is to relate the new knowledge given to the educand to the old knowledge he has received. This helps the educand to assimilate the new information.

Locating difficulties: The only way of finding out the student's difficulties in learning a subject is to ask him questions. This is essential, because without removing difficulties, teaching cannot be effective.

Test of knowledge: One set of questions can be specially devised to test the knowledge that the individual educand has grasped so far. It is believed that greater accuracy in the answer of one educand than of another, indicates a better grasp of what is being taught. In our own examination system, questions are asked for this purpose.

Cooperation and active participation of educands: If the lecture on any subject is interrupted frequently to ask questions to the educands, they are compelled to attend to what is being said and perforce to remember it also. Hence, educands are asked to answer questions in order to ensure their active participation in teaching.

Means of development: Asking questions can also be the means of the intellectual and social development of the child. Social development depends on asking questions and receiving answers, because this increases mutual contact. If educands are permitted to ask questions freely, it helps in their free development.

Localising around the basic lesson: Another objective of asking questions is to localise or concentrate the subject matter around the basic subject. It sometimes happens that the educator wanders from the subject he is teaching. In such a situation the question asked by the educator or the educands once again focus his attention on the subject matter.

Practice and repetition: Another reason for asking questions is to allow the educand to apply his knowledge. In answering questions, the educand has to make use of the information he has acquired and this helps him in retaining it.

Practice and repetition: Yet another aim of asking questions is to repeat the subject, matter and give the educands practice. The text books prescribed for various levels of education are equipped with a set of questions at the end of each chapter. These questions are intended to provide practice and repetition. That is why these questions are frequently entitled 'questions for practice'.

Encouragement to thinking and observation: Sometimes the questions are deliberately framed in such a way that the answers to them cannot be found either in the educator's lecture or in any text book. In order to answer them the educand has to depend upon his observation of things, objects, individuals and surroundings which form part of his environment. He is also compelled to think about such things. Such questions have particular importance when they are used to encourage independent thinking and originality of ideas. Educands with a greater degree of creativity rarely need such stimulus for they are in the habit of observing things of life and thinking about them.

Increase in self-confidence: This method has the advantage of adding to, the educand's self-confidence because when he answers questions successfully, he realizes that he has understood and learnt the lesson.

It is clear from the foregoing account that this method of asking and answering questions is valuable both for the educator and the educand. It is not essential that a particular question must have only one specific reason behind it. It may be motivated by a number of reasons, even a few of which have not been included in the preceding account.

Important Factors

Apart from the aims and the language of the question, the manner in which it is asked is also significant. If the manner of questioning is faulty, the question will not fulfil the purpose for which it was asked. Hence, in asking questions, the teacher must remember the following points:

Seriousness: Questions should always be asked seriously. It is improper to laugh, show anger or smile when asking questions.

Attracting attention: Questions should be asked to arrest the educand's attention when it shows signs of wandering away from the subject being taught.

Proper frequency: The frequency of questions should be so managed that they should not be too far apart in order to avoid lassitude or disinterest and not so close together as to give the educand no time to think at all.

Proper interval: The interval between questions can be determined by the complexity of the subject matter and the intelligence of the educands.

Proper distribution: Questions should be distributed over the entire lecture so that students are compelled to attend to each part of it.

Entire class: Questions should be asked to the entire class so that every individual is forced to exercise his mind.

No side issues: Questions should not be prefaced with side issues, they should be clearly stated so as to avoid wastage of time.

No repetition: Questions should not be repeated as a matter of habit. If this is done, educands do not pay attention to it the first time, confident that it will be repeated. It should only be repeated as an exception, not as a general rule.

Neither too simple nor too difficult: The subject matter of the question should conform to the knowledge and intelligence level of the educand, neither too simple, nor too difficult. If the questions are too simple, they will not require any mental effort, while excessively difficult questions will cause excessive strain on the educand's mental faculty, without achieving the desired result.

Varied form and language: The form and language of the questions should be varied in order to bring in variety and avoid monotony and disinterest.

Collective thinking: Even if the question has been satisfactorily answered by the first educand, the educator must continue to ask the same question to the other educands so that all the aspects are clarified by the thinking of all the educands.

Encouragement: The question should be accompanied by repeated comments which encourage the students to answer the question. This builds up the confidence of the educands and makes them feel that they can answer the question if they try.

Proper language and subject matter: The language and subject matter of the question should be determined beforehand. If the educator repeats the same question in different words, it creates the impression that either the educator has no self-confidence or that he has made no preparation. In both the cases the impact on the educand is undesirable.

It is clear, therefore, from the above description, that the questions should be carefully, asked, keeping in mind the language, the style, purpose, etc.

Traits of Proper Answers

In this technique of asking and answering questions, the answers are just as important as the questions. On the one hand, it is essential that the questions should be presented in the best possible way, and on the other, it is equally important that educands should be trained to answer questions properly. In the modern examination system, the educand's character, ability, mode of thinking, knowledge, in fact, everything is judged by the answers that he provides to the questions asked in the examination. Hence, the educator must train the educand to give the right kind of answer, and in order to do this, he himself must be aware of the qualities a good answer must possess. The following are these qualities:

Appropriateness: The first quality of a good answer is that it must answer the question without going into long and purposeless digressions. But the answer can be appropriate only when the educand's ideas are clear. Lack of clarity in ideas communicates itself to the answer and makes the answer inappropriate.

Completeness: When the answer is complete, it helps the audience or the reader understand the subject. Hence the words used in the answer must convey the same sense to the listener that they convey to the user, the sense in which the latter has used them. Incomplete answers should not be accepted. The teacher must insist upon the educand's completing his sentences and providing a complete answer.

Linguistic qualities: Language is the medium in which answers are given and in order to make language intelligible it is necessary to follow certain rules of grammar. Hence, the language of the answer should be grammatically correct. Besides, it must also be simple and clear, because there is no virtue in using difficult language. The only purpose in answering a question is that the answer should provide the information which is being called for. And since language is a medium of expressing ideas, the educand must be trained in the correct use of language so that he can express his ideas with clarity and precision. As far as possible, the language of the answer should be pure not mixed with a large number of obsolete or uncommon words or foreign expressions. Again, the educand should be taught to avoid hyperbolic language because his aim is not to impress the listener with his command over the language. But the use of long and crude words should also be avoided, and in answering questions economy of expression should be exercised. Verbosity, again, is no virtue.

Order: The answer must also have properly ordered parts, the arrangement being determined by the order of the various parts of the question. If the answer is not properly ordered, it cannot be said to be good or accurate.

Quickness: When questions are being asked verbally, there is some value in the answer which is made rapidly and quickly. If the educand takes unnaturally long time in answering the question, this detracts from the merit of the answer.

Proper tone: The proper tone also plays a vital role in the answering of questions, because an unusually high tone has a bad effect on the listeners. Hence, there is no need for the educand to shout his answer, just as much as there is not any need to speak in an inaudible whisper. The educator should train the pupils to answer questions in an even and balanced tone of voice.

Illustration Technique

In the illustration technique of teaching, a subject is explained by providing examples of facts or experience of which the educands are already aware. In this technique is implicit the principle of proceeding from the known to the unknown. Very often concrete illustrations and examples are used to explain some abstract idea or theory. In this is implied a progress from the concrete to the abstract. In the same way many known facts are cited as example to help the educand to understand facts of which he is as yet unaware. The principle underlying this situation is the progress from the known to the unknown. In each case, the real aim in providing an illustration is to create an association, the right background for presenting new knowledge. This method of teaching has many advantages, among which are the following:

Advantages

Overcoming difficulties: Illustrations and examples help to overcome the difficulties faced by the educand in understanding the subject. Thus, his ideas are clarified and he is enabled to understand something which had eluded his comprehension.

Assists in elaboration: Illustration help in the explanation and elaboration of abstract concepts and many scientific principles, because verbal explanation becomes more concrete so that the complex subject is somewhat simplified. For this reason, teaching by illustration is considered essential for the teaching of many sciences.

Encourages interest and curiosity: Illustration tends to increase the educand's interest in the subject and to enhance his curiosity to know more about it. In the absence of interesting illustration, the teaching of science becomes drab and monotonous. Illustrations also provide the correct distraction for the student so that the process of learning becomes interesting and compelling.

Helps memorizing: Illustrations not only help in teaching and understanding but also in memorizing or retaining subject. It helps recall because concrete facts are easier to memorize and recognise than abstract ideas.

Assists observation and experimentation: The presence of numerous illustrations during a lesson sharpens the educand's observation. Besides, the teaching of many sciences is done through experiments which serve as illustrations.

Types of Illustrations

1. Non-verbal, natural, objective or concrete illustrations
2. Verbal illustrations.

Under the first category we have :

(i) Analogies,

(ii) Comparisons,

(iii) Similes,

(iv) Word pictures, etc.

This depends upon :

(i) The nature of the subject

(ii) The level of pupil's development.

Lower the classes, the more profitable will be concrete illustrations. As the child grows and his intellectual level rises, one can use pictures, diagrams, sketches, graphs, etc. Verbal illustrations such as analogies and similes, etc, should be used with children with a higher level of intelligence. They should be used with pupils at the secondary and higher secondary stage.

Proper use of illustrations

Simple: Use simple illustrations. They should be easily understood without any need of comments and explanations.

Relevant: Use illustrations which are relevant to the topic.

Best: Do not use too many illustrations in a single lesson. Only a few and best should be used to illustrate a lesson.

Proper occasion: Use illustrations at the proper time during the course of the lesson. Do not lay out a number of illustrations on the table before the class, just in the beginning of the lesson.

Illustrations are a good antidote to verbalism. Wisely selected, exhibited with timing and intelligently and tactfully used, illustrations prove a great asset to teaching civics.

Home-Work

This is another technique which can prove helpful in teaching civics to the students of secondary and higher secondary classes.

Home-work gives opportunity to pupils to plan and perform their work independent of the guidance and help of the teacher. Pupil's ability improves by the better use of books and resources outside school. It stimulates voluntary effort in the pupil to follow up the study of topics or units that appeal to his interest and accustom him to revise and consolidate the work done in the school.

In civics, home work may take many forms. Students may supplement class-notes with brief notes from or reference to text-books, standard books upon the topic or unit. They may prepare detailed notes from specialist sources. Essays may be given as homework, either as answers in examination or more exhaustive accounts.

Home-work may also be in the form of projects. The pupils should work on the projects, keep up diaries, scrap books and news cutting from books.

The teacher may also set simple problems from work books or assign multiple-choice questions. The students may be asked to prepare charts, graphs, posters, maps, etc, connected with different topics of civics.

While using home-work as a technique in teaching civics, the teacher should try to set a task interesting in itself and making intellectual demands on the pupils. Home-work should not be made too hard or too long. More time will be spent on it if the work is interesting.

Carefully organised, intelligently assigned, properly understood and regularly checked Home-work is invaluable in the teaching of civics.

Notes

Notes Taking

There are few things the teacher of civics can do for his pupils which will be of greater practical use to them than to teach them how to take notes. Notes-taking is useful in education and life. The pupils need to take notes both from the lessons or lectures they listen to and the books and periodicals they read. Notes provide a permanent record and afford easy reference.

To be permanent, the notes are to be well-written and well set out. Pupils should be asked to rewrite the class lessons to give them proper shape. To serve the purpose of affording quick reference, notes need to be well set out under headings and sub-headings and sub-sub-headings.

Dictation of Notes

Preparation of notes should be a work of the student. Dictation of notes is not a desirable practice though there is no harm if quotations and some of the definitions are dictated. Notes should be the unique product of the mind of the teacher and the mind of the taught.

The teacher should give guidance to the pupils in the art of note-taking by writing on the Black board the numbered or lettered headings and sub-headings of what he intends to talk about during the lesson. This will lay down guidelines and the students can develop their own notes under the headings. The essay type material should not be given under the headings. It is to be analysed into separate numbered or lettered points.

Preparation of Notes

Right from the earlier classes the pupils should be guided in the preparation of notes. At the early stage, the teacher may give a skeleton framework for a lesson and ask the pupils to write a few sentences of their own under each heading. Later, the pupils may be put to work on making detailed notes according to a provided scheme of headings. They may be encouraged to go in for some collateral reading. It is advisable to suggest the sources from which the required material is to be collected. The pupils should be encouraged to prepare their own notes about such complicated topics which call for greater display of their wits, critical and reasoning faculties as Five Year Plans, India and the World, India as a nation, State and National Government, Democracy in India, etc. More importance should be attached to the way in which the notes are organised such as their page headings, cross references and table of contents. Checking the notes prepared by pupils the teacher will be in a position to put his finger on the pulse of the pupils in matters of extra reading.

Assignment

Assignment is a very useful device of teaching civics, particularly to the pupils in secondary and higher secondary classes. Some significant topic or sub-topic is assigned to the pupil for preparation, study, revision or remedial work. The pupils are required to prepare the assignments in writing. Written assignments help in organisation of knowledge, assimilation of facts and better preparation for examinations.

Types of Assignments

Preparatory assignments: This preliminary pilot work is meant to prepare the pupils for the work to follow on the next day. It enables the teacher to lead the class with ease and understanding.

Study assignments: The study assignments vary with individuals- each according to his need and each according to his capacity. These can be- Problem-solving Assignments, Assignments on making charges, graphs, tables etc., assignments for the preparation of a topic in the light of references provided, assignments for listing points in favour or against a given argument, reading valid conclusions from statistical or visual data, etc.

Revisional assignment: These assignments are given for

(a) providing drill to the work done by the students,

(b) checking their retention and reproduction of the facts of the topic or unit, and

(c) checking the understanding of the topic.

Keeping in view the specific objectives of the subject-matter being tested, these assignments need to be worked out in advance.

Remedial assignments: Devised in the light of pupil's reactions to the three types of assignments mentioned above these assignments remove weak points and clear misunderstandings.

Traits of Proper Assignments

The civics teacher should bear in mind the following points in making assignments:

Motivating pupil effort: Students need good reasons for doing things. As they want to see the pertinence of the assigned work to their concerns, problems and needs, it is necessary for the teacher to relate the assigned work to the pupil's present needs and stimulate related interests.

Related to purpose: Assignments must be pertinent to the goals of instruction. The teacher should help students understand the learning objectives and recognize the relationship of assignments to them.

Challenge, not punishment: Assignments can be challenging if they are meaningful and promote student involvement. Assignment should never be given by the teacher as punishment.

Provide for individual differences: As students differ in interests, aptitudes and abilities, some provision for individual differences is desirable. An assignment is too difficult for some and too easy for others. The civics teacher should divide the class into subgroups and provide appropriate assignments for different groups. Differentiated assignments should be made, the quantity and quality of work expected for various grades may be indicated and the student may be allowed to choose and work towards the grade he wishes.

Co-operatively made: Both the teacher and the taught should to be actively involved in assignment. The student is doing the work for his own benefit. He should have an opportunity to contribute to the sort of assignment he is supposed to work on.

Not to be lightly tossed of as the final bell sounds: A vital part of teaching assignments require serious consideration and thoughtful planning. If well planned, the assignments can promote serious learning.

Assignment is a useful device of teaching civics. It helps the teacher know the interests of the pupils and to foresee the difficulties which the students may have to face in the learning of the topic. The teacher can guide the pupils by putting thought-provoking questions in his assignments. The guidance to read or to study a topic prepares the pupils to face the difficulties.

Supervised Study

Meaning

Supervised study is one more useful device of teaching civics.

While the people work at their desks on the assignment given to them, the teacher supervises them. When the pupils find a difficulty they cannot overcome, they ask the teacher for direction and assistance. The teacher is always available at the pupils desks, watching the pupils do their work, continually on the alert for any wrong procedures that they may follow. He is always ready to direct and help them. Maxwell and Kilzer have aptly defined supervised study as the effective direction and oversight of the silent and laboratory activities of pupils. Supervised study is a directed study procedure. The pupils learn certain skills essential to successful use and understanding of civics content under the supervision of the teacher. As the teacher gets an opportunity of observing the pupils from a close quarter he can be of considerable help in more ways than one. Pupils benefit from his attention. This brings to the situation that knowledge of each pupil is accumulated from observation. He can detect a pupil's habits, efficiency of study skills and degree of progress. At the spot guidance proves very useful. As the errors are corrected at once pupil's time is saved enabling the teacher to redirect his efforts.

Advantages

Democratic relations: Supervised study encourages democratic human relations. Pupils learn to share materials, to wait their turn and to understand their own difficulties. This develops a sympathetic attitude towards the difficulties of others. Aware of individual differences, teachers become guides.

Guidance: As the teacher supervises each pupil, who proceeds slowly, he goes into effective learning experience guided by teacher's questions or suggestions to overcome difficulties. The discontented pupil can be given a more satisfying interpretation. The pupil who works more rapidly and requires a greater challenge to use his ability can be further motivated to put in his best.

Effective use of learning material: As the teacher constantly supervises materials like books, reference books, charts, maps, etc, these can be used more efficiently. The pupils learn the specific types of information available in various reference books.

Developing better pupil-teacher relations: Instead of being a hard task master the teacher is a helper and a guide displaying sympathy and understanding. Able to understand the pupil and his difficulties he is in a position to spur him on to greater effort.

Critical thinking and discrimination: The supervised study is useful in establishing habits of critical thinking and discrimination in evaluating ideas and in objective investigation of facts on the part of pupils. It encourages the pupil to compare facts and to evaluate their sources. He learns to withhold his opinion until enough evidence is available to justify a conclusion. Thus, pupils learn to examine the material critically which is a valuable experience.

Maxims of Teaching

From the known to the unknown: The most natural way of teaching a lesson in civics is to proceed from something that the pupils already know to the facts they do not know. Old knowledge serves as a hook on which the new can be hanged. To make the new knowledge acceptable, the civics teacher must try to win over some part of the child's past experience to act as host on which ideas, sensations and impressions can be apperceived or assimilated. An attempt has to be made to remind the pupils of what they already know so as to be ready to pin the new knowledge on it. The civics teacher must search diligently to find which of pupils experiences have been such that by recalling them, he is likely to ensure a ready welcome for the new knowledge.

In teaching a lesson on India and the United Nations, the teacher may ask the pupils to describe the organs of the UNO and the various attempts made by it to bring peace in the world and then introduce the pupils to the contribution of India in UNO.

From the simple to the complex: The civics teacher should divide the lesson in such a manner that the ideas which are easier to understand are used as a starting point and the difficult ones follow in the proper order during the lesson. 'Simplicity' and 'complexity' should be determined from the pupil's point of view. While teaching any topics of civics, the teacher should begin with the most striking and prominent features of a topic, and then continue to add further details. While teaching a lesson on Social and Economic Reconstruction to the VIII class students, he shall tell that what is needed to be done is removal of poverty, checking increase in population, meeting the problem of unemployment, etc. He should analyse each issue and discuss it in detail.

From the indefinite to the definite: While vagueness characterises the early ideas of the pupils, the aim of teaching is to make ideas clear and precise. This can be done by making pupils interested in the lesson, and take an active part in learning. Good teaching of civics necessitates that every definition, concept, idea discussed in the lesson stands out clearly in the pupil's mind. The use of pictures, charts, graphs, films, filmstrips, analogies, comparisons, etc., should be frequently made to clarify ideas and make them definite.

From the concrete to the abstract: The civics teacher should try to teach his subject in a psychological way. He should be careful about the suitable arrangement of the subject-matter and the child's nature. He should be fully conversant with the requirements of the syllabus and understand the pupil's interests, needs, reactions and mental make-up. There should be psychological selection of the matter to be presented. Then he can logically arrange the matter into sequences and steps. The civics teacher should proceed from the concrete to the abstract, from the simple to the complex, from the known to the unknown. In really good lessons on civics, pupils are gradually made to learn difficult facts in a very easy manner.

From empirical to rational: Empirical knowledge is based on observation and first-hand experience while rational knowledge implies abstraction and argumentative approach. The child has the rational basis for any knowledge much after he has experienced it in his day-to-day life. In civics teaching, Local Self Government would make better sense, if it were taught in the practical context of everyday life, instead of in the format of abstract theory.

QUESTIONS

1. What are the main techniques of civics teaching? Describe question-answer technique.
2. Explain and evaluate Home-work as a device of civics teaching.
3. Explain the maxims of civics teaching.
4. Describe briefly the various techniques of teaching Civics.
5. Describe fully how you would make use of the modern techniques and suitable aids in the teaching of Civics.
6. Give an account of the different techniques of teaching civics. Also state which of the technique is the best and why.

6
Teaching Principles

For successful Civics teaching, it is essential to know how the pupil learns and by which methods he learns. The teaching methods or strategies are based on certain principles. Therefore it is essential for a Civics teacher to follow these general or basic principles while teaching:

General Principles

Principle of motivation. Motivation is the method which creates pupils' interest in the content. The principle of motivation is to create interest in the pupils for acquiring knowledge. It is a psychological fact that the process of teaching and learning goes on smoothly when a teacher motivates the pupils to acquire knowledge. In the absence of proper motivation, the pupil takes no interest in memorizing the contents. Hence the Civics teacher should follow the principle of motivation. How are the pupils prepared to gain knowledge? For this, the civics teacher should use the pupils' innate tendencies, for example, as the pupil is very much curious to know about the new things regarding environment, the civics teacher should create such situations in which a curiosity is aroused in the pupils regarding the acquisition of the latest knowledge concerning the novel things and contents about the social environment.

Principle of activity of learning by doing. The principle of learning by doing means that the civics teacher should create activity in each type of lesson. This activity is of two types- (1) Physical, and (2) Mental. The physical activity means to activate in the body organs of the pupils, while the mental activity means to activate the sense organs of the pupils. Temperamentally each pupil is active. This activity should be in accordance with his nature. According to

McDougall, every child has inborn instinct of construction due to which he remains busy all the time in doing some or the other activity. The more the activity of the pupil, more would be the teaching-learning process. Therefore, for a successful teaching of civics the teacher should make use of the pupil's instinct of construction. The maximum use of the pupils' basic instinct at the time of teaching will make the teaching effective to the maximum: Both, the physical activity and mental activity depend upon each other. As the pupil's mind and body work together, he shows more interest in learning something new. The eminent educationist Froebel has called this principle learning-by-doing. The principle of "learning by doing" does not mean that the pupil himself should only be active for learning by doing, but it also means that the teacher should also make the pupil active for learning the new things. For example, while teaching civics the pupils can learn the historical facts and incidents concerning citizenship very conveniently if these are shown in the form of Plays as compared to the learning from books. Good feelings arise in the pupils by keeping themselves active.

Thus, the principle of activity should be used in each class and in all the school activities, such as — school council, declamations contest, various societies, meetings, conferences, clubs and games, etc. This will develop social habits in the pupils and they will get proper and sufficient training of social service.

Principle of interest. The principle of interest means to create interest of the pupils in the subject-matter in order to make the teaching useful and effective. When the interest of the pupil is created in the subject-matter, he acquires knowledge very conveniently. He faces no difficulty while studying. There are various methods for creating interest of the pupil for example— (1) Curiosity of the pupil should be aroused and the objective of the, lesson should be made clear. The clarity of the objective to both the pupil and the teacher creates the interest of the pupil for the lesson, (2) The civics teacher should establish a relationship of contents with the pupils' activities and objectives, (3) The principle of learning by doing should be followed, (4) The teaching should be linked with the active life of the pupil.

Principle of linking with life. The pupil at each level has his own world. As he grows, he begins to imagine his world in his own way. He shows his interest in those subjects or activities which are linked to his personal world. Keeping in view this thing, the activity and the subject should be linked with the learner's life. The principle of linking with life means relating the subject-matter with the life of the pupils. The pupils show interest in learning those things only which are expected to be used in their future life. They learn rapidly and conveniently those things which get related to their life. According to Ryburn, "Life is a continuous experience. Everything we do is linked up with what has gone before and with what comes afterwards." Out of childs daily experiences, only those get stabilized which have some relationship with his or her previous experiences. Therefore, it is necessary to relate the new experiences with previous experiences. After a relationship between new and old experiences, the new experiences or knowledge become a part of the pupil's life.

Principle of definite aim. Every lesson must have some definite aim or objective. In the absence of an objective, the teacher is like a boatman who has no knowledge of his aim and the pupil is like an oarless boat which is sailing in the sea-waves blindly. Therefore, there must be some definite, clear and completely defined objectives in order to make the lesson interesting and impressive. The objectives and the teaching methods are closely related. Every teaching method is based on some objective. The teaching method should be used according to the objective. For example, if our objective is the creation of the traits of good citizen, then its method would be entirely different from that method which has an objective of teaching a poem to the pupils. Full knowledge about the objective provides success to the teacher in his teaching task and the interest of the pupils is created in the lesson.

Principle of recognizing individual differences. Psychological researches have proved that the pupils are not alike in intelligence, nature, ability, interest, potentialities and needs. Each pupil is not at the same level. In order to develop all the pupiis for equal opportunities, the teacher should impart proper guidance to the pupils, sympathy should be shared with the abnormal pupils, and in order to bring the mentally retarded and backward pupils to the Formal level, affectionate behaviour should be exhibited. Thus the teacher should maximize the development of all the pupils on the basis of individual differences.

Principle of selection. There is a close relationship between the contents and the objectives of education. The contents are selected according to the objectives. Since the human being appeared on this Earth, he has collected huge and complex knowledge. If a teacher wishes to impart the knowledge to the pupils without considering any definite objective of education, it would be a serious mistake. Some things are essential and some are non-essential. The non-essential things confuse the pupils. Hence, the teacher should select only those facts which the pupils can understand in order to achieve some definite objective. He should sclect what and how much is to be taught to the class. He should select the content according to the definite, clear and predefined objective. This benefits both the teacher and the pupils. The teacher develops the lesson successfully and the pupils acquire knowledge conveniently.

Principle of planning. The teacher should ascertain the teaching sequence and the lesson-plan should be prepared after proper planning. This enables him to solve every problem concerning teaching. He should decide how much cooperation of the pupils he can seek in order to solve a problem with the help of which method and at what stage before preparing a lesson plan. A problem may arise at the time of teaching which had never been imagined. In such a situation, a teacher should solve the problem immediately in accordance with his ability.

9. ***Principle of division.*** The subject-matter should be divided into some units for presenting it in certain order. The division of the content should be followed by the presentation in such a manner that

each unit should seem to be complete in itself. One unit should create curiosity for other unit. By presenting the contents after dividing it into units, the lesson becomes very easy for the pupils. They acquire knowledge easily without any difficulty. By not doing so, the lesson becomes complicated and the pupils fail to understand anything. Hence, for a successful teaching of civics the division of the lesson into an order of units or steps is necessary.

Principle of revision. Whatever subject-matter is taught to the pupils, it should be revised by them. Revision is very much essential in learning. Without experiments and revision, everything is forgotten. Therefore, the acquired knowledge should be revised by the pupils not only immediately, but also it should be used repeatedly. The frequency of the revisions depends upon the nature of the lesson. Hence, the more difficult, the lesson is more its revisions should occur.

Principle of creation and recreation. Activities are carried over by the pupils which are recreational and which can develop the creative power of the pupils. This will create interest in the pupils regarding the teaching activity without any fear of the teacher and the school. They will try for new innovations. They will have an opportunity of expressing creative activities. The principle of recreation is very essential for successful teaching. In civics so many teaching methods have been developed which are based on the principles of creation and recreation or learning by play-way.

Principle of democratic dealing. While teaching civics the teacher should adopt democratic attitude with the pupils. He should not be dictatorial. Dictatorship instigates the pupil's for revolt. In a democratic set-up, every pupil is considered as a holy and valuable member of the society. He gets maximum opportunities for developing his self-thinking and independent expression in order to develop his personality. As the modern age is democratic the teacher should adopt democratic attitudes for the pupils. It means the development of the lesson with the help and the cooperation of the pupils. The teacher should ask maximum questions and the pupils should be allowed to remove their doubts. This creates the habit of thinking independently and the pupils develop self-confidence, self-esteem and self-respect, etc.

Psychological Principles

These psychological principles are used for making the learning process effective. These principles are as follows :

Principle of motivation and interest. The motivation and the interest have been considered most important in the teaching-learning process. Both the teacher and the learner should work with interest and motivation.

Principle of recreation. If the pupil feels fatigue in the class it creates boredom in the pupil and he shows disinterest in the task. Hence, the principle of recreation should be followed in the class.

Principle of repetition and exercise. The process of forgetting starts due to the disuse of the acquired knowledge. Hence, repetition and exercise should be followed in the class daily.

Principle of encouraging creativity & self-expression. To encourage the creativity and self-expression is the duty of the teacher. He should develop the habit of innovations in the pupils. The pupils should be capable of presenting their views and attitudes.

Principle of remedial teaching. If there are errors in the pupils and the teaching activities, the teacher should identify these errors and provide remedy to his erroneous teaching activities. This task is not so easy. The teacher has to overcome many obstructions.

Principle of sympathy and cooperation. If a teacher exhibits sufficient sympathy for pupils and contributes in overcoming their difficulties, he can be a good guide to the pupils.

Principle of reinforcement. The term 'reinforcement' is concerned with making the learning process effective. In teaching process, the reinforcement is the utilization or presentation or removal of such stimuli that the possibilities of recurrence of any response increases. For example, if a teacher gives some reward to the pupils for correct answers, the possibilities of the similar behaviour from the pupils increase.

QUESTIONS

1. Describe the general principles of civics teaching.
2. 'In teaching, interest is the main word.' Throw light on the principles of creating interest in the pupils while teaching civics.
3. What is the importance of activity in civics teaching?
4. What do you mean by the principles of teaching? Describe general and psychological principles of teaching civics.
5. How are the general principles of teaching helpful in teaching civics? Support your answer with proper examples.
6. What do you mean by the psychological principles of teaching? Explain briefly various principles useful in teaching-learning in civics.
7. What is meant by psychological principles of teaching? Explain the implications of such principles in civics.

7
Significant Values

Values are the ends or the objectives that are achieved by doing a thing. Teaching of Civics is done with the following values in mind :

1. Character-formation.
2. Development of the qualities needed for an ideal society.
3. Development of the outlook of the citizens.
4. Hygienic outlook.
5. Proper use of science.
6. Knowledge of political problems and development of capacity to solve them, and
7. Social outlook.

Character-formation. After making a thorough study of the structure of the secondary education in India, Mudaliar Commission on Secondary Education in its report, has tried to give due place to various subjects in the curriculum. While talking about the importance and the value of teaching of Civics, it has said that it leads to character formation. The teaching of civics brings about the development of the qualities of co-operation, kindness, sympathy, shouldering of responsibility, etc. These qualities have great value in the social set up.

Development of the qualities needed for an ideal society. Teaching of Civics brings about the development of the qualities necessary for an ideal social set up. Civics helps children to understand the complex society. The spirit of co-existence, and spirit of 'Live and Let Live' can be acquired only through the teaching of Civics. This quality is very much needed for an ideal society.

Development of the outlook of the citizens. India is faced with various social problems like untouchability, illiteracy, low status of women, etc. These problems can be solved only if the citizens develop a scientific outlook in regard to these evils. Teaching of Civics is useful in the development of such an outlook. It helps the citizens in the solution of these problems.

Hygienic outlook. The teaching of Civics enables the young men and women to acquire a hygienic outlook. Hygienic outlook is the realisation of the fact that 'sound mind lives in the sound body'. Once a citizen has realised this fact, he tries to give a practical shape to various principles that bring about good health and sound physique.

Proper use of science. Our's is an age of science. Various inventions have been made that can lead to the annihilation of human race. Once a man has developed the outlook of a world citizen, he shall not try to employ science for the destruction of the human race. Teaching of Civics develops such an attitude.

Knowledge and capacity to solve political problems. Teaching of civics enables a citizen to acquire knowledge and capacity to solve various political problems. He tries to apply healthy principles in the political life leading to development of a healthy political atmosphere, which is a great boon for a democratic set up.

Social outlook. Man cannot flourish unless the society flourishes. The teaching of Civics enables a young man to acquire a social outlook. It helps him to realise that the proper working of the society can bring about the real pleasure. With this outlook, he tries to play an active role in this direction and tries to raise the society higher.

Democratic Values

Aldous Huxley has remarked, "If your aim is liberty and democracy, then you must teach people the art of being free and of governing themselves." Democracy can never be successful without education. Wherever democracy has been unsuccessful, it has been because of the lack of education. In a democracy the government is composed of the elected representatives of the people and if the people are uneducated they can never elect the right leaders and consequently can never create the right kind of government. In fact, it is impossible even to hope for democracy in the absence of education. It is difficult to expect a citizen to have responsibility if he is not even aware of his rights and duties. Bertrand Russell has commented, "Democracy in its- modern form would be quite impossible in a nation where many men cannot read." The truth of the matter is that education is a prerequisite for democracy. Only after proper education should the citizen be invested with his democratic rights. As Fichte, the German philosopher has commented, "Only the nation which has first solved in actual practice the problem of educating perfect men will then solve the problem of the perfect state." Although Fichte made this comment in the context of autocratic state it can be judged only by the extent to which it contains educated people. As Hetherington puts it, "Democratic government, at least, demands an educated people." Throwing light on the objectives of education in the 1949 meeting of the Universities Commission, Dr. S. Radhakrishnan stressed the fact that the democratic state recognizes the importance of the individual, and it is the process of development of this individual, which is called education. Hence, education is absolutely necessary for establishing a democratic society. Dewey has pointed out that democracy is inconceivable without education, because education alone can generate and instill the qualities which democracy demands as a prerequisite. Philosophers of the ancient Greek city state were aware of the significance of education. Both Plato and Aristotle laid stress on the importance of education for the success of democracy. Ernest Barker comments, "To Plato education was the most important function of the state and the department of education the most important state department which was particularly advocated for producing the philosopher kings to improve the men's minds for becoming virtuous beings." Plato, in his famous text, *The Republic* stressed not only the importance of education for democracy but even formulated a plan for the education of men and women which made all kinds of development physical, mental, moral and aesthetic possible. Aristotle was of the opinion that the aim of the state is to make possible the achievement of the highest moral level and this can be reached through education alone. Thus, education is the most important function of the state. From one point of view, the state itself is a school in which the individual learns citizenship, for Aristotle suggested that the aim of education was to produce good citizens. These truths were known not only to the ancient Greeks but also to Indian thinkers of ancient times. India has been the home of democratic ideals and principles from ancient times. Hermitages and places of worship were used as schools in which the sages tried to produce ideal citizens who could become useful members of society. But the modern age needs democratic education far more than was needed in ancient Greece or ancient India because modern democracies are so vast and their problems so complex that the education of citizens is even more imperative today.

Education for Democracy

All these important aspects of democratic education hold true in India also. India is not merely a modern democratic state but a country which is traditionally inclined towards democracy. A democratic constitution was adopted after Independence. In 1938, Jawaharlal Nehru had said, "The Indian National Congress stands for independence and a democratic state". This objective was achieved after Independence with the establishment of a democratic society. The Indian Constitution seeks to establish a popular government in the country on the basis of democratic principles outlined earlier. For this every citizen must participate in the administration, through his right to vote and to be elected. Every individual is guaranteed and given equal status and opportunity, because no one is discriminated against on the basis of religion, race, caste, community, sex, or on any other grounds. The government is responsible to the people and its elected representatives.

In order to achieve this objective of democracy, education is as necessary in India as anywhere else, a truth which the Indian people have been quick to realize. In the words of Dr. F W Thames, "There has been no country where the love of learning had so early an origin or has exercised so lasting and powerful an influence. From the simple poet of the Vedic age to the Bengali philosopher of the present-day there has been an uninterrupted succession of teachers and scholars." Not only did the Indian Constitution accept the ideals of democracy, it considered education the prime responsibility of the state. In Article 45 of the Constitution it has been stated that every state must arrange for the provision of free and compulsory education to all children up to the age of 14, within ten years of the date of inception of the Constitution. After the achievement of independence, a new phase began in the history of education. Articles 29 and 30 of the Constitution give fundamental rights to every individual in connection with education and cultural development. According to Article 29, every Indian national living in any part of India will have the right to maintain his own specific language, script and his culture. No person can be refused right of admission to any educational institution, established by the state, by reason of religion, race, caste, language or any other similar consideration. According to Article 30, every minority community will have the right to establish and maintain educational institutions of its own choice, irrespective of whether the minority is a linguistic or religious one. The state will also not refuse aid to any such institution created by a religious or linguistic minority. Articles 45 and 46 determine the policy for education as part and parcel of the directive principles. According to Article 45, the state will make efforts to provide free and compulsory education, within ten years, to every child below the age of 14. According to Article 46, the state will pay special attention to the educational and economic interests of all backward classes, especially the Scheduled Castes and Scheduled Tribes. It also entrusts the state with the duty of protecting backward classes from social injustice and exploitation of every kind. The Indian Constitution laid the foundation for a federal government in which the functions of the state and central government are distinctly defined. Both the central and state governments have some duties with respect to the education. It has been realized that there must be coordination between the central and state authorities on education for a balanced development of the country. The modern Indian state is a welfare state whose objective is the complete development of its people. This welfare can be achieved only through education. Little surprise therefore if all the leaders of the nation stress the importance of education as a first step to improve the future of the nation.

Democratic Objectives

The democratic ideals which the existing educational policy is trying to achieve are outlined most precisely in the Secondary Education Commission's explanation of the objectives of education.

Development of democratic citizenship. The success of democracy depends largely upon the people's awareness of their rights and duties and the extent to which people fulfil their responsibilities. Education aims at developing this ability in the people, because education teaches the man to think and distinguish between right and wrong. He can understand social, economic and political issues and reflect on the possibility of solving such problems. He can decide upon the political party or the leadership which should be entrusted with the task of forming a government and undertaking administration. He does this thinking of the problems facing the country and considering the ability of each group or leader to face such problems. He can express his ideas and suggestions through lectures, essays, articles, etc. He can organize new movements or constitute various kinds of committees to solve the problems facing the country. It is the duty of the state to insist upon a syllabus which can be expected to generate such democratic awareness among the children being educated.

Training in skilful living. Democracy can be said to have succeeded only if , it can translate the democratic ideals to its society. And, for this, socialization of individual through education is essential.

It is desirable to develop such social qualities as collective feeling, cooperation, discipline, tolerance, sympathy, brotherhood, etc., in the individual. Education must also aim to create faith in social justice and willingness to rebel against injustice. Education helps people in adjusting to each other, and the educated individual is generally tolerant and liberal. Although he may differ from other people in their opinions, he has the ability to adjust to such people because he can understand their attitudes. Hence, education is the only means of removing the obstacles in the path of democracy, and also of achieving some adjustment between people who differ from each other in respect of language, race, caste, religion, sex, etc.

Development of personality. The success of a democratic society also depends upon whether mature men and women form the majority or minority in its population. Democracy can succeed only if most of its members have developed mature personalities, because a mature person has gone through physical, mental, social, ethical and spiritual development. And education is nothing more than this comprehensive development. Hence, education should aim at the development of all aspects of the educand's personality through various kinds of training. Keeping this in view, most schools and colleges now provide many kinds of extra-curricular training, which supplement all that is taught as part of the curriculum.

Developing Vocational skill. The Secondary Education Commission has pointed out that another aim of education is to develop some vocational skill in the educand. No nation can progress in the absence of economic progress. The first duty of the state is to provide a system and means of educational skill to the educands so that they can earn their livelihood at the same time as they contribute to the nation's economic growth. The country urgently needs skilled craftsmen, engineers, doctors, teachers and administrators. For this, specialized colleges are required. Every child should be given the right to choose a profession of his own liking, and opportunity to acquire the highest training and education in this profession.

Developing leadership. The success of a democracy depends upon the capabilities of the leadership. The democratic government is a decentralized government, for that reason it requires skilled leadership of administration. The democratic government is run by the elected representatives of the people who should possess special qualities. Expert leadership is required for development and progress in every sphere-political, social, economic, artistic, scientific and cultural. Education should aim at evolving such leadership because without doing this education cannot make any real contribution to democracy, for, then it is leaving unfulfilled one of its important responsibilities.

The element of leadership can be encouraged through many kinds of curricular and extra-curricular activities in schools.

Apart from these objectives of education laid down specifically by the Secondary Education Commission, it is desirable to reflect upon some other objectives, which have significance in view of the fact that India is a democracy. In fact, the aims of education vary a little bit with the level of education- the primary, secondary and university education- a fact which has been recognized by the different education commissions established from time to time. The aims of education, at the primary level, is to develop the child's mind by presenting the fundamental elements in the various areas of knowledge, and also to give him an opportunity to develop all his abilities- physical, mental, moral, motor, creative imagination, etc. At this stage attention should be paid to physical development no less than mental development, but attention must also be paid to the burden such an education places on the child. The education imparted should not become a burden.

At the secondary level, attention should be focused on discovering the interests and abilities of every adolescent, and then developing such abilities. Education should be concerned not merely with the general welfare of society but also with the self-realisation and personal development of each individual.

Emotional Integration

The consciousness of nationality is generated in the younger generation through education, and hence there is a profound relationship between nationality and education. In India, when the revolt against the British government was awakened all national leaders demanded the formation of a national educational programme. They argued that the educational programme of the country should be modified to suit the requirements of the nation. In 1921, Mahatma Gandhi expressed his views on this subject in *Young India,* criticising the existing educational pattern introduced by the British people. He too demanded that the educational pattern must be modified to suit the demands of the nation. His reasons for adding manual work to education were sound since he knew that education must pay its own way in a poor country like India. Rabindra Nath Tagore conducted an experiment in Shanti Niketan to produce a novel kind of human society in which the problems of the individual and the community, the nation and the world, could be solved simultaneously. Swami Dayanand insisted upon reforming education to suit the educational pattern that existed in ancient times. On the other hand, Annie Besant's educational plan, which included the establishment of primary schools, lower middle schools, higher middle schools, high schools for general education, high schools for general science, commercial schools, technical high schools, agricultural high schools, etc., was more directly in touch with the problems of contemporary India.

Madan Mohan Malviya established the Hindu University at Kashi in order to realize the ideals of education which prevailed in ancient India. In addition to these individual and specific efforts, all other educational philosophers of the time, including Sri Aurobindo, Vivekanand, etc., favoured the modification of the educational pattern in order to make it conform to ancient Indian values, ideas and thinking. In more recent times, in his report of the Universities Commission, Dr. Radhakrishnan pointed out the defects of the existing pattern of education, and suggested that it should be refashioned to fulfil national needs. It is only because of the feeling of nationality that most educationists have objected to the use of English as a medium of instruction in the country. Everyone has stressed the need for education to be a character building process, because without this the future of the nation will always remain dark. Dr. Radhakrishnan has said that the future of the nation is made by character. No country can be great if its inhabitants have low character. If we want to create a great nation, we must educate our young men and women in such a manner that they should possess the force of character. We must have men and women who see themselves reflected in other human beings. This has been said in our sacred texts.

Stressing the need for an education for nationality, the Kothari Education Commission has said that the objective of our system of education should be to develop national consciousness. For this we must develop the knowledge of our cultural heritage, but we must also submit this cultural heritage to revaluation. At the same time we must have faith in the future towards which we are moving.

Nationalism in the New Generation

The following suggestions can be given for generating nationalism in the younger generation :

Development of a national language. The first prerequisite for developing nationalism is the development of a national language in the country. In India, this position can be occupied only by Hindi. When the succeeding generations learn Hindi and use it, the feeling will gradually take root that India is one nation.

Development of a national literature. Development of a national language will lead to the development of a national literature. With the propagation of Hindi in every part of the country, a new literature will be created, which will be read everywhere. Apart from encouraging national unity, it will also enable the people to create a literature which encourages national power and protects the cultural heritage of the country.

National educational programme. In India the spread of education is the responsibility of both the central and the state governments but as yet, it has not been possible to formulate a national programme of education, with the result that one can see considerable disparity in the various parts of the country. In order to evolve a feeling of nationalism the country should have a unified educational programme which should be flexible enough, to take within its purview the differences that exist between one region and another. This will lead to a certain similarity in the education in all parts, and make possible the application of a single curriculum through which national literature on the all India scale can be created.

Observance of national festivals. The feeling of nationalism can also be strengthened by enthusiastic observance of national festivals, Independence Day, Republic Day, Children's Day, Teacher's Day and the birthdays of all great men.

Respect of national symbols. Another way of fostering the feeling of nationalism is to generate and show respect for national symbols such as the national anthem, the national flag, the national bird, etc.

Improvements of curriculum. In order to help the development of the national sentiment, it is desirable that the teaching of civics should be conducted in such a way that it helps national sentiment. This can be done by preventing the publication of any material in text-books and other media of publication which hurts national sentiments and pride. The government should seize all copies of such material and punish the publisher and authors.

Cooperation of political parties. It is impossible to generate nationalism if the political parties fail to cooperate. Many political parties not only hinder the growth of this sentiment, but actively engage in activities calculated to harm the national interest. Such political parties owe their allegiance to other nations, show no respect for national symbols and spread anti-national feelings among the people. As far as possible, political parties should be prevented from indulging in such activities.

Cooperation of teachers. Education for nationalism can never be really successful without the active cooperation of teachers. For this reason, the educators must themselves possess this feeling, because then they can set an example for the educands. It will then be even easier to grow the national sentiment among the younger generation.

Nationalism and Internationalism

Nowadays many thinkers object to the use of education for fostering the national sentiment because they have come across many bad effects of narrow nationalism in many countries and seen that education for nationalism has stood in the way of the growth of internationalism. The education for nationalism that was given in Italy and Germany, for example, was completely opposed to internationalism. It is in connection with this one-sided education that Bertrand Russell pointed out that children are taught to exhibit complete devotion and worship to the state of which they are citizens. The lesson taught to them is that worship of the state consists in doing as directed by the state. For this they are taught distorted versions of history, politics and economics so that they should not be critical of the blind national faith expected of them. They are acquainted with the evil actions of other nations but not of their own although the truth is that each nation has been unjust to other nations. It is unquestionably true that if the facts of history are distorted in order to propagate the sentiment of nationalism it is undesirable. But this danger is not peculiar to nationalism alone. It is true of almost all human relations that as they become deeper and stronger they also become narrower, and that they impede the growth of any liberal attitude. If, for example, an individual has intense love for his family, this may come in the way of his loving his nation, but this does not imply that love for nation can exist only at the cost of love for family. Proper and healthy love for the family does not impede love for the nation, it helps it to grow. In the same way healthy nationalism also does not preclude the possibility of internationalism. As Dr. Louise has said that it is essential to strengthen one's love for one's motherland, but this does not make it proper to violate the canons of humanity, for the external benefit of one's own nation. It is obvious, therefore, that education must not only propagate nationalism but must also encourage internationalism. The plan for national education presented by such eminent educationists as Mahatma Gandhi, Sri Aurobindo, Vivekanand, Ravindra Nath Tagore, etc., has kept this in view, that nationalism and internationalism should grow harmoniously. That is the reason why Rabindra Nath Tagore's Shanti Niketan turned into an ideal institution for education in internationalism. According to Tagore the educand's aim is to reach the level at which there is no distinction between nationalism and internationalism.

International Understanding

In order to encourage the growth of internationalism, it is necessary to make suitable amendments and modifications in the objectives of education, in the syllabus, and in the methods of teaching., The following suggestions have been put forward :

Aims of Education

With the intention of spreading international feeling, the following aims of education should be paid special attention :

Development of independent thinking. Education must help every student to think for himself so that he should not blindly accept every statement favourable to his own country, and blindly reject everything in favour of another.

Developing a feeling of world citizenship. Education must also seek to teach children that they are citizens of a world state. When this feeling is developed in them, they will have no difficulty in rising above national interests and understanding international interests, which they will try to achieve.

Creating faith in humanity. Rabindra Nath Tagore, the strongest supporter of internationalism among the contemporary Indian educational philosophers, based his concept of internationalism upon the philosophical background of humanitarianism. Humanity is the true religion of human beings, while all the great religions are only its different forms. All great religions have placed great stress upon the equality of human beings. Human perfection has been accepted as the goal of human life. Once this concept is understood, it becomes easy to have faith in humanity and to love all human beings irrespective of their country.

Syllabi

The following changes in syllabi are suggested, if an international feeling is to be created

1. All syllabi should include paintings, literature, music, etc., which are typical of different countries.
2. The children should be acquainted with all attempts at humanitarian work carried out in every part of the world.
3. Efforts should be made to overcome narrow-mindedness and blind faith in children through a scientific education.
4. The teaching of geography should be supplemented with knowledge of the singleness of the world.
5. The teaching of history should concentrate primarily on the efforts of great figures who have contributed to the history of the world.
6. In teaching civics, the educator should explain to the student not only the rights of citizens but also the rights and duties of a person to the international community as a whole.
7. Teaching should not be restricted to bookish teaching alone, but must also extend to visits to different parts of the country and also to other countries.
8. Pen-friendship should also be encouraged.

Methods of Teaching

Certain suggestions about the changes and improvements in syllabi also imply some changes in teaching methods, if education is to have an international impact. The points to be noted in this connection are :

Stress on world citizenship. During the process of teaching, it is desirable to stress points which may help in evolving an all encompassing love and world citizenship.

Stress on similarities. The teaching of history, geography and civics, should concentrate not upon the differences between and tensions among nations but on the similarities so that sympathy for other nations and nationals is awakened in the mind of the educand.

International viewpoint of educator. But an international viewpoint cannot be generated in the educand if the educator himself lacks it. When the educator is possessed of it, he will inspire the educand through his conversations, his ideas, training, and by setting an example. Hence, the first step in the process is to educate the educator.

International contact. The various committees for the various sciences and arts that are constituted at the university level should be encouraged to develop contact with national and international institutions of the same kind. What is really required is international contact at all levels of life and among people of every walk of life, scientists, scholars, literary figures, teachers, doctors, in fact, every profession. Such contacts can be evolved by international meetings of local committees concerned with different professions, and also through mutual exchange of scholars and learned people.

Finally, it has also been suggested that every national plan of education in every country, must make a specific provision for developing international feeling through education. Educators and educational institutions should be given specific instructions concerning this. Only this will awaken sufficient enthusiasm in local institutions, and only thus can the aim of international education be fulfilled.

QUESTIONS

1. What values are taught through the teaching of civics ?
2. Show how civics teaching is education for democratic values.

3. Show how teaching of civics may be helpful in increasing national emotional integration.

4. How can civics teaching develop nationalism in the new generation? How would you synthesise nationalism with internationalism ?

5. Discuss civics as education for international understanding.

8
Subject Matter Organisation

Organisation of the subject-matter in Civics teaching is essential in order to teach it in an effective and coherent manner.

Different Approaches

The following approaches may be adopted for organising the subject-matter of civics

1. Concentric Approach
2. Topical Approach
3. Unit Approach.

Concentric Approach

According to this approach, children in the primary classes begin to develop simple generalisations about man carrying on his everyday activities. As they progress through the middle and high classes students work with more and more difficult arrangement of information, and, deepen and reshape the dimensions of their generalisations about these activities. By the time they complete the secondary stage, they refine the same generalisations many times, using increasingly more abstract levels of thought at each higher echelon of learning. In civics teaching an attempt is made to design a sequential arrangement of experiences that will produce a spiral of cumulative learning. Areas of study at each level are treated holistically Whatever is taught to the child is a whole in itself though scope for additions should be made with the addition of understanding and maturity. For instance, boys and girls should know India's freedom struggle. In the primary classes, the information about this unit will be imparted through some of the more important leaders. In the middle stage, the information will be imparted through events — the Indian National Congress, partition of Bengal, the Gandhian era — Civil Disobedience, the INA, Quit India Movement etc. In the secondary stage, the pupils will, learn to compare and contrast the freedom movement in our country with other countries of the world. They should know about the United Nations and its role in international peace. In the primary classes, they will know something about the importance of cooperations among nations, work of UNICEF, WHO; UNESCO, India in the U.N. In the middle classes again, information will be provided about the need for cooperation, co-existence, the United Nations, etc. In the secondary stage, more information will be imparted about international peace and cooperation and the role of India in the United Nations and the world. Thus, as the child advances in age and understanding, he can think in more abstract terms. Learning is continuous and unbroken through the primary and secondary stages. The learning sequence progresses from the simplest unit to the most detailed in gradual stages.

Thus, concentric approach is devising a strategy that fosters continuous, unbroken learning of the subject-matter of civics through the primary, middle and secondary stages.

In this approach, while the path is narrower, the way is simpler ; the pupil gets somewhere and will not easily forget his journey. As he is interested from the very beginning, it is easy to proceed from the known to the unknown.

Use of this approach will make civics a subject of immediate and real interest. For the average pupil, it will be the basis of an abiding interest. For the more intellectual, it will be the basis on which higher studies can be built.

Limitations

This approach is criticised on many grounds :

(i) This approach is psychologically unsound as the same facts are repeated again and again. Being devoid of freshness and novelty the presentation inevitably fails to rouse curiosity and a sense of wonder in the pupils.

(ii) In this approach, it is difficult, if not impossible, to give a clear picture of a problem vivid with detail. Hurried and passing references will not be of help in understanding complex problems.

(iii) It is difficult to develop time and space sense in the pupil's in this approach.

(iv) In this approach the joy of discovery, the freshness of events, the adventures and achievements of great personalities, the atmosphere of an age or era, the constitutional landmarks are denied to the children in a strictly concentric approach to civics. A sense of boredom and dullness is inevitable because they have gone through the whole course more than once. They develop a sense of familiarity without the fullness of knowledge.

This criticism can be met by making the repetition interesting by following a different approach and a fresh point of view in different stages.

Topical Approach

In this approach, certain topics of study suitable for the age, ability and interest of children make up the whole syllabus. Each topic stands by itself and all the topics are connected together by the teacher with the help of individual lessons called 'link' lessons. For the children of the age group 13 + and above, topical approach is quite worthwhile.

According to the topical approach, the curriculum maker takes particular topics as the central theme of work in civics at different levels of instruction. The nature of the topics vary in accordance with the age, ability and interests of the children. In the primary classes, the child may start the study of the developments of means of transport. In the middle classes, they may be introduced to more important and more difficult topics such as the history of government. The development of the topics is traced; the topic supplies the central theme from which subsidiary investigations can radiate as far as pupil's time and intelligence allow. Several events are logically and intelligently related.

By a careful selection and detailed study of the topics, opportunities can be provided to the students- for an intensive study of a particular problem. Instead of repeating the content a number of times the teacher can discuss all the aspects of a problem and give an overall view of that particular problem.

Advantages

(i) This approach provides a solution for dealing with a vast material in a logical and rational fashion. It helps the pupils to understand the facts in their developmental setting. This is the only approach by which civics could be studied through considerable stretches of lines without grossly overloading the syllabus establishing at least a foothold in ancient societies, while at the same time, maintaining a connection with them here and now.

(ii) The topical approach can be adapted according to the age, ability and aptitude of the children. This flexibility is of special significance when we think of projects on topics pertaining to' transport and communication, government, etc.

(iii) The study of civics through this approach imparts a sense of purpose to the pupils. They are clear about what they are studying.

(iv) The topical approach enables the teacher to control the subject-matter and adapt it to the varying needs of the students. As there is a definite problem before the pupils the consequent study shows an intelligible objective, *i.e.,* understanding the problem in all its facets.

If the topics are selected wisely, and the treatment is interesting, the approach can prove useful in teaching civics in all the stages-primary, middle and secondary.

Unit Approach

Of the various ways of organising material in civics courses, the unit approach predominates in popular usage. The grouping of related lessons into about ten to twenty or more major topics, provides a tangible aid both in planning instruction and in comprehending the scope of the course of civics.

Definition of Unit

Dictionary of education. Unit, "is an organisation of various activities, experiences and types of learning around a central problem or purpose, develops cooperatively by a group of pupils under teacher leadership ; involves planning, execution of plans, and evaluation of results."

I. Hanna, N. Hageman and G. Potter. 'A unit can be defined as purposeful learning experience focused upon behaviour of the learner and enable him to adjust to a life situation more effectively."

E. S. Johnson. "Unit is a segment of experience which is cut out for study ; within it, method is employed. It is my understanding that every unit is a *project.* It is a project in the sense that one projects inquiry into it. Furthermore, every unit has a *topic, theme or central tendency* or whatever name you choose to call it, otherwise it could have no unity. Every unit is a *contract in* the sense that the student enters upon a contract or obligation to study how the things, which it contains, are related, how they work, how cause and effect are identified and related, and how a conclusion is reached. Every unit is also a *problem:* a problem of significance and meaning in some unknown or less than thoroughly known phase of human experience."

John Jarolimek. "A unit is a means of organising materials for instructional purposes which utilizes significant subject-matter content, involves pupils in learning activities through active participation intellectually and physically and modifies the pupil's behaviour to the extent that he is able to cope with new problems and situations more competently."

Characteristics

Experience: It is purposeful learning experience, having significant content, comprehensive enough to have scope and unity.

Involvement: It involves pupils in learning activities through active participation intellectually and physically.

Development: It develops certain information, understandings, attitudes, interests and skills to enable the pupils to cope with new problems and situations more competently.

Types of Units

Resource unit. It is a teacher's guide to planning and action, a blue-print of suggestions and resources for developing a theme, problem or topic. Regardless of former structure, it includes the following elements

(i) Statement of objectives related to a theme

(ii) Problem or topic

(iii) An approach or initiation

(iv) Content or subject-matter basic to the area of study

(v) Direct and related experiences

(vi) Organising and summarising experiences

(vii) Evaluation of learnings, and

(viii) A collection of instructional resources.

Teaching unit. It is used to describe the development of a unit of work in the class-room. Referred to as the unit in action, it focuses on implementation, learning activities and processes that take place as the unit develops. The areas of learning and the sequences in it may or may not be prescribed. However, the needs, the maturity level and the background experiences of a particular group of children set the boundaries of the teaching unit and determine its direction.

A resource unit contains an organised collection of teaching ideas and suggestions built around a large topic of significance while the teaching unit contains definite plans for teaching a specific group of children under a given set of circumstances.

It should be: A Good Unit

Topical: It should deal with a sizable topic.

Appropriate: In terms of the child's understandings, interests and capabilities it should be of appropriate difficulty. A variety of activities, materials and modes of expression are essential for meeting individual needs so that each child gets opportunities to make worthy contributions to the achievement of group purposes.

Variety of material: It should allow the use of a variety of materials and activities like community resources, audio-visual materials, dramatic play and excursions, map-making, chart making, planning, discussing and evaluating.

Reading material: It should allow use of sufficient amount of book and other reading materials.

Suitable to the maturation level of the children: Units should be of shorter duration in the primary classes. In middle and high school classes than those in the primary classes the units may last a few days to a week or two. Higher class children may engage in a single unit for several weeks and continue to find themselves in a challenging, interesting situation.

Evolutionary or functional: It should be based upon the principle of a process. Whatever the field or aspect, it must move towards something to show development or evolution.

Connected with past experiences: It should emerge out of the children's past experiences and lead to broader interests, an integrated learning experience and the continuity of the child's learning.

Creative: It should provide opportunities for creative experience like expression in art, dramatic play, poems, stories, songs, etc.

Steps in Unit Planning

Objectives: Objectives may be clearly stated, in categories like 'knowledge', 'understandings', 'skills', 'attitudes', 'interests'. They must be achievable and make the teacher conscious of the process of teaching.

The theme: It enables the teacher to get a clear background of the whole unit and focus the attention of the teacher on the main points of teaching.

Subject-matter**:** It should be selected with care and arranged in proper order and sequence.

Pupil's activities**:** It suggests the learning aspects of the educative process. The teacher may suggest some of the activities essential for learning civics. These may be of varied types such as activities in the class-room, outside the class-room, individual activities, group activities, etc.

References: References for the guidance of teacher's need should be given from books from their libraries along with a list of films and film strips.

Teaching aids: Different types of teaching aids may be utilized for the proper teaching of a unit.

Teacher's remarks: *These* should be serving as guidelines for others in the implementation of units in other classes. These may include suggestions regarding the total number of periods necessary for the unit, and other points which may prove helpful to other teachers.

Advantages

Suitability: In the words of Jarolimek, "The extension of knowledge and the development of skills, abilities and attitudes are all possible outcomes of good units". Well suited for the growth and development of the abilities and skills attendant to democratic behaviour, ideals and processes Unit, afford limitless possibilities for the development of critical thinking, problem-solving, planning, consideration for others, responsible habits of work, listening, discussing, reporting and experimenting.

Facilitation: The organization of experiences and materials into units facilitates the child's learning significant relationships, concepts and processes. Acts learned in their proper context are remembered longer.

Adaptation: Because of its flexibility the unit provides facility in adopting instruction to individual differences of children. It rejects the notion of fixed, uniform standard of achievement. It substitutes the concepts of continued progress and growth for individual children. Unit planning focuses attention on the individual child, his chief concerns, problems and interests Standards of achievement are kept at a high level. They are also different for each child. The structure of the units facilitates meeting the educational needs of individual children.

Need satisfaction: As distinct from the requirements of the content the needs of the learner are given top consideration providing for varied experiences, activities and opportunities for the development of the child.

Focusing attention: Focusing attention upon significant results the unit avoids the confusion- and discouragement from long attention to insignificant details.

Useful division: As it is impossible to study every thing at once, Unit is a logically useful division cutting out a field or phase of study.

Selection of the Teaching Material

Proper organisation of the curriculum is required for achieving the aims and values of the teaching of Civics. Teachers have to look towards the various informations and the subject material, whose organisation may lead to the achievement of the aims and objectives. Though this is a difficult task, it is on the basis of which, the subject material or the content material of the civics may be organised.

Flexibility: Man is a dynamic being with activity as an essential part of his personality. He continues to progress higher and higher. He has to struggle hard with the circumstances to face the difficulties of life. As he has to adjust himself as well he requires elasticity or flexibility. It is through flexibility that he is able to establish his superiority over other beings. Through struggle with the circumstances he gains certain experiences which are given place in the curriculum. This is helpful in acquiring further knowledge. When the present experiences are correlated and connected with the past experiences, it is easy to acquire further knowledge. If the link that is established is weak, one cannot make the knowledge stable and permanent. Therefore, it is the duty of every person, interested in education, to preserve the experiences of the past. The values of the past provide a foundation to the child, to build his own super-structures of the values. Therefore the past experiences are given a place in the curriculum. This can be done by the curriculum framed on the principle of flexibility.

Activity: Educationists believe that 4 H's should find a place in the curriculum: Health, Head, Hands and Heart. A coordination should be established between the hands and the mind. It would enable the children to act intelligently. Child is active by nature. His path of activity and agility should be free from difficulties. The organisation and selection of the subject material of Civics should be based on activity. Such events, instances and topics of Civics that lead to the activity in the child should be included in the curriculum. The curriculum should be so organised that it may bring about activity in the children.

Utility: Ours is a world of selectivity. In regard to subject material and activity we follow the principle of pick and choose. Subject material of Civics which fulfils our educational needs shall be useful.

Educational Life

Whitehead has classified the educational life into three stages-(1) Romance, (2) Precision, and (3) Generalisation. Here precision is nothing but utility. Selection of the subject material of civics should be based on precision and utility. Material that is not precise and useful should not find a place in the teaching of Civics. With the development of various mental powers, the child is able to discriminate between useful and useless, welcoming what is useful and discarding what is not useful. If the content material of teaching civics is not based on the principle of utility, it shall not attract the students towards the study.

***Formality and cultural heritage*:** In India, each individual is proud of his or her cultural heritage. Indians try to preserve the culture handed over to them by their forefathers. Along with it we also try to enrich it. This can be done by including the teaching of civics in the curriculum. Civics should be taught through the subject material that helps preservation of culture and its enrichment. This may be done only if the subject-matter is selected on the basis of the principle of formality.

***Interest*:** Interest, aptitude and other mental faculties play a vital role in the child's education. Hence attempt is made to base the entire education on the interest of the children. Subject material selected should be of interest to the students. The teaching of Civics should be so organised that it is interesting to the educands. If the content material is not based on interest, children shall not be inclined to study it. Modern education is child-centred. Therefore, to organise the subject material of the civics, one must keep his eye on the interest of the child. The selection and organisation of the subject material should be according to the nature of the child.

***Principle of selectivity*:** A teacher cannot teach each and everything in the curriculum. He has to follow the principle of pick and choose. Things that are helpful for the betterment of the society and bring about the preservation of the social values and cultural standards are given place in the curriculum of civics. The content material has social and political problems. The material should be in tune with the intelligence and mental power of the students. .

Concentric growth: According to this principle the teacher should proceed 'from known to unknown' and 'from concrete to abstract'. First of all, those facts should be presented before the child that are already known to him. Then facts unknown to him may be presented. While teaching Civics, first the problems dealing with the local aspect of citizenship should be presented before the children. Then should be presented the national and international problems appertaining citizenship.

Widening circle: Initially a child lives in the family. As he grows first he comes in contact with his neighbourhood, then in contact with the town, the state, the country and the entire world. The knowledge and the teaching of Civics should begin with the knowledge of the family. The teacher should try to present the ideals of citizenship before him as it affects his family. He should gradually broaden this circle of knowledge to arrive at citizenship of the world or world citizenship.

Organisation of the Facts

In constructing curriculum or laying down the subject material of teaching Civics the teacher faces the problem of organisation of the facts. These should be so organised that the students may acquire and assimilate them thoroughly. Following principles have been laid down as principles of organisation of the facts

Integration: The selected content material of teaching of Civics should be integrated and co-ordinated with the curriculum of Economics, History, Geography and other branches of social studies to enable the students to think that various subjects are interdependent and coordinated. They should be given a thorough knowledge of other subjects.

To be systematic and well-ordered the integration should be so organised, that the content material, that a student studies in one class, should not be repeated in his next class. The teacher should remember that in higher class the student should get higher knowledge about a thing that he has studied in the lower class. This shall make the knowledge of the students systematised and organised. A systematic integration will help the students to learn the subject material easily and thoroughly. With such a process of integration he shall have a thorough knowledge of the subject.

Solid or concrete circumstances: While organising the content material of teaching civics the circumstances and the conditions in which the child lives, should form the foundation to help the child to grasp the subject material easily and quickly.

Individual interests and aptitude: The organisation of the content material of civics should be based on the interests, aptitude and mental faculties of the children. If it is organised to suit the interests and the aptitude of the children, it shall be useful and helpful for them.

Co-ordination of the knowledge of one subject with other subjects: In the scientific way of education the content material of the Civics should be so organised that it is co-ordinated with the knowledge of other subjects.

Presentation of the Subject-Material of Civics

Following are the various stages of education according to the Secondary Education Commission:

Primary stage. This includes classes I, II, III, IV and V in which the students of the age group of 6-11 years come to receive education.

Junior High School or Pre-secondary stage of education. This includes classes VI, VII and VIII in which the students of the age group of 11-14 years receive education.

Secondary stage of education. It includes classes IX, X, XI and XII. Class XII is not included in the secondary stage of education.

University stage of education. It includes the teaching of BA., B.Sc., B.Com., MA., MPA., M.Sc., M. Com., etc., and also research work.

Presentation of subject-material of civics is concerned only with the first three stages of education.

Principles of the presentation of the subject-matter: Following are the basic principles that the civics teacher has to bear in mind while presenting the subject-matter of civics before the students of the first three stages of education :

Matter. The matter presented should be factual and intelligible.

Individual differences. The teacher should try to present the subject-matter with an eye on age, mental growth, needs, interests and aptitudes of the students.

Practice. As theoretical presentation of the subject-matter alone is not enough for a civics teacher, stress should be laid on the practical importance of the knowledge.

Teacher's conduct. As children are prone to imitation in the earlier stages, the teacher of civics should present material before the students in such a way that they may do such things that are good for civics education and the work in the class. This means that the conduct of the civics teacher should form an ideal for the students.

Co-ordination. It is the essence of teaching of Civics. The teacher should try to correlate the subject-matter of Civics with life to help the student to use the subject-matter in their practical life.

Scientific method. In order to follow the scientific method of teaching, the teacher should try to proceed from simple to complex and from concrete to abstract.

Primary Stage

Children of 6 to 11 years of age group are taught at this stage. As they are fresh from the family life, an attempt should be made to conduct their life in such a way that they may develop the social qualities, which shall be helpful for their future life.

Curiosity is the basic instinct at this stage of life. Children of this stage are very fond of listening to stories as they have a lot of curiosity. The teacher should base his presentation of the subject-material on the basis of curiosity. He should utilise this instinct of the students and their fondness for listening to stories, in presenting the subject-matter in the form of stories. The teaching should be through the story method.

Selection of Stories

Activity. The story may develop the activity of the students.

Interests and Mental age. The story should be in accordance with the interests and mental age of the children.

Nature of story. The story may be historical as well as imaginary.

Ideals. Every story shall present one or the other ideal of Civics.

Precautions in presentation of material

(i) The teacher should not use the text-book very much at this stage of education. Books utilised should be profusely illustrated.

(ii) *Simple and Natural.* The nature of the story should be simple. The teacher should to narrate it in a natural manner and at a speed that the students may follow it. Short sentences should be used.

(iii) *Practical.* The students should be given practical education as far as possible.

(iv) *Development of Civic Qualities.* Civic 'qualities should be developed in the students through stories. An attempt should be made to develop those qualities and habits in the students that may be helpful in their practical life.

(v) *Discipline*. The training of the discipline may be imparted to the students through drill method or exercise.

Use of the Black-board. At this stage black-board should be used for explaining the pronunciation of the names to the students. Too much use of black-board shall not be useful. The teacher should write out very legibly on the black-board. If the teacher writes in a good hand witing it shall encourage the students to imitate it and also improve their hand-writing. The students should be given the training of expressing their ideas. Excursion, trips and tours shall also be helpful to impart the training in civic virtues.

Use of Dialogues. In attempting to teach the principles of Civics through dialogues, these should be very short but interesting in the lower classes. The dialogues may be of one to two minutes of duration. These should not be carried out for more than 10 to 15 minutes.

Use of charts, maps, pictures, models, etc. These teaching aids make the lesson interesting while teaching Civics. The teacher should use these things in the class room. He may also encourage the students to copy these things. Only essential things should be taught to the students at this stage of education, as far as possible.

Pre-secondary Stage of Education

At this stage of education the students of the age group of 11 to 14 years are taught, who are slightly grown up children. They are not very much fond of listening to stories. They are actually heading towards maturity and adolescence. They no more live in the world of imagination. At this stage, they start using their power of thinking and reasoning. Therefore, fairy tales cannot be interesting for them.

Hence, the teacher should change his course of action and method of teaching. He should keep an eye on the developed brain, vocabulary and the knowledge of the students. The subject-matter should be presented to them in a practical manner.

Story method. Story method can be used at this stage but it should not be of the type that is used at the primary stage of education. The story should be of slightly developed nature so that it may develop certain civic qualities in the students.

Other methods. Observation, narration, question-answer, project and dramatic methods may be employed at this stage of teaching civics.

Tour and excursions. The teacher should take the students out on tours and excursions and make them see the working of Municipalities, Corporations, Panchayats, Zila Parishads, etc.

Text-books. It is useful to employ text-books at this stage. These text-books should not be read out in the class. They should be used by the students at home for revising the lessons that they have learnt in the class room.

Supplementary reading material

Supplementary reading material may also be used by the students.

Practical Work

The students should also be encouraged to take to practical works. These should be directed towards ideals of teaching of Civics.

Black-board. As compared to the primary stage of education black-board should be used more at this stage. The teacher should draw sketches, maps, graphs, etc., on the black-board. He should explain the topics to the students with the help of these tools. The students should also be encouraged to come and write on the black-board.

Models, charts, maps etc. All these tools should be used at this stage of education to strengthen the experience of the children. The students should be encouraged to draw these tools themselves.

Radio and Films. Radio and films may also be used at this stage of education.

Home work. Home work should begin at this stage of education. The teacher should ask the students to do some home work. He should himself examine the home work with interest. If the teacher is interested in the home work the students shall also be interested in it. Most of the teaching should be oral though written work must start at this stage.

Secondary Stage of Education

At this stage of education the teacher has to deal with adolescents, in whom the power of reasoning, thinking, arriving at decisions, etc., have developed. Their physical development is fast and considerable. The teacher should take the interests, aptitudes and the talents of the students into consideration. He should organise his teaching, with an eye on these elements.

Besides the physical development Self-Regarding Sentiment develops, at this stage of education. The teacher should not insult the students. On the other hand, they should be encouraged to do things in a way that they receive appreciation from the members of the society.

Moral development takes place by this time. Vocabulary also grows rich. The teacher should utilise these developments for the benefit of teaching Civics.

This is called the Age of Organisation'. The various talents and faculties of the children start organising themselves. The teacher should arrange his teaching with an eye on this aspect of the personality.

Use of Text-books. Text-books should be compulsorily used at this stage. The students should be encouraged to repeat and revise their class room lessons at home with the help of the text-books. They should be encouraged to prepare notes with the help of the text-books. The teacher should ask them to write out answers of certain questions, which may encourage and awaken their mental powers.

Self-study. The students should be trained in the art of self-study. They should be asked to go to Library and select out good books themselves. The teacher should help them in this task.

Discussions. At this stage students should be encouraged to take part in discussions and debates. Such discussions may be organised in the class room. Discussions and debates will improve the power of thinking, reasoning, etc.

Participation in School Activities

The students should be encouraged to undertake tasks of responsibility in the school. They should be encouraged to form voluntary student bodies and take part in student's Government. These organisations should be so directed that they take up healthy activities to generate and strengthen the civic qualities of the students and prepare them for their future life.

Use of Black-board. Black-board should be used sparingly. The teacher should put down substances and other short notes, while students should be encouraged to develop that substance in the form of essays, etc.

Teaching aids. Models, charts, maps, etc, should be used to make the lessons interesting. Tape recorders, radios, films, newspapers, magazines, etc., may be used to add to the knowledge of the Civics. The teacher can make his subject material interesting with the help of these things.

At this stage of life, as students are very fond of roaming about, excursions to places of civic importance will add to their interest and knowledge of Civics. They should also be acquainted with the current events of social, political, religious and moral importance. They should be encouraged to take active interest in gathering information about all aspects of life. An attempt should be made to make civics teaching practical as far it is possible.

QUESTIONS

1. What are the different approaches of organising the subject matter in civics? Discuss the merits of each.
2. What do you understand by a unit? Discuss the unit approach with all its merits.
3. Discuss the potentialities of unit method as a method of organising the subject-matter of civics.
4. "Concentric approach of organising the subject-matter is better than the unit approach." Discuss.
5. What do you understand by topical approach of organising social studies? Suggest list of topics which you can take up in the context of IX class in teaching civics.
6. Describe briefly the principles, on the basis of which the subject material of the teaching of Civics is selected and organised.
7. What principles would you bear in mind while selecting and organizing the subject matter of civics?
8. Describe briefly the method of presentation of the subject material of Civics at various stages of education.
9. Discuss the presentation of subject-matter of Civics at different stages of study.
10. What principles would you bear in mind in presentation of the subject-matter of Civics at different stages? Discuss.

9
Process of Evaluation

The Radhakrishnan Report of 1948-1949 hinted at the social aims of colleges when it said that the educational institution should introduce the educand to community life, provide useful information, and help to develop the necessary habits of intellectual work. It was also indicated that the current pattern of education did not fulfil our social requirements. The following shortcomings were noticed

Lack of Objectives

The prosperity of any nation depends upon the success of its system of education. The education in a country should conform to the national interest. From this standpoint, Indian education, particularly higher education, is entirely inadequate. Most educands receiving higher education were not aware of the reasons for receiving it. As a consequence, this aimlessness led to indiscipline, lack of sociability, etc., and also made it difficult for the educand to play a useful role in society once he had left college.

Defective Syllabi

The current system of education was rendered obsolete because the syllabi had not been brought up-to-date. Consequently, the education provided through them could not possibly satisfy the contemporary needs of our society.

Miseconomy

Concerning the uneconomic performance of higher education, the Universities Commission had commented that a very large quantity of public funds were being wasted every year. What was even worse that this miseconomy involved a further waste of the time, effort and money of the parents of each student, and yet achieved nothing better than a total indifference to the frustration of the student's ambitions and hopes. This misuse of public funds is proved by the fact that there are larger number of educated unemployed in the country than uneducated unemployed. Evidently, if this education cannot train a man to earn his own livelihood, it can hardly be expected to turn him into a social asset.

Specialization

Modern education pays little attention to comprehensive and all round development of the educand. Higher education provides him with considerable information on one subject, but also deprives him of the opportunity of finding out anything about any other subject. As Mr. K.G. Saiyeden has remarked, a narrow-minded unimaginative specialization leads to students of science being completely ignorant of art and poetry and students of the arts being incapable of understanding how science and scientific methods have transformed the world in which they live. But it cannot be forgotten that it is difficult for such one-sided personalities to adjust in society. Such individuals find it difficult to fulfil their responsibilities devolving upon them from a variety of social relationships. For this reason, specialization in education hinders the fulfilment of social needs.

English as the Medium of Education

Considered from the social standpoint, education in India can claim to be a success only if it produces individuals who are capable of having a sense of oneness with their countrymen, rich or poor, educated or uneducated, villagers or city dwellers. This can be done only if education is imparted through the mother tongue or' the national language. But since English is the medium of instruction in many states it leads to an alienation between the educated and the average Indian not similarly educated. Gandhiji also commented on the role of English as the medium of instruction in India. He said, "To inflict English on children is to stunt their natural growth and perhaps to kill originality in them." He also remarked that it had sapped the nation's power, weakened people, separated them from the common mass and made education unnecessarily expensive. The harm done to country by this education is only too evident.

Defective System of Examination

The system of examination at every level of education : primary, secondary, intermediate, university is very defective. In fact, it does not provide any real clue to the ability of the educand. It indicates nothing more than his ability to memorize bookish knowledge, of which it is an adequate test. It does not suggest the level of development he has achieved. Consequently, the educated individual possesses a fund of knowledge, but his personality does not develop.

Encouragement to Individualism

Modern education encourages the spirit of individualism and leads to the expression of such anti-social traits as indiscipline, obstinacy, irregularity, misuse of authority, sexual misbehaviour, etc. It is seen that the uneducated individual is possessed of more social sense than the educated. Such an education is not only inadequate but positively harmful for society.

In view of the above shortcomings, the defectiveness of the present system of education and its failure to satisfy current social requirements need hardly be debated further. Very few, if any, educated people evince any desire for social service. On the contrary, the more educated the individual, the greater is his selfishness, pretension, egoism. If education is to serve the ends of society, it must get rid of the, shortcomings outlined above. After India achieved her independence, a number of commissions appointed for the purpose of reviewing the system of education have pointed out the above defects time and again. The government has done something to eliminate these defects, but an educational system which will satisfy our society's requirements is a far cry. For this it is essential that the system of education must conform to the requirement of the nation.

Meaning of Evaluation

Evaluation is an all inclusive concept. It indicates all kinds of means to ascertain the quality, value and effectiveness of student's knowledge. It is a compound of objective evidence and subjective observations. It is the total and lineal estimate, a valuable, an indispensable guide to the modification of policies and action. It is the approval of pupils progress, in attaining the educational goals set by the school, class and himself.

The chief purpose of evaluation is to guide and further the students learning, evaluation is a positive rather than a negative process.

Importance of Evaluation

There is a need to measure student's achievement in every aspect of life. The measure of achievement is known as evaluation or examination. Unless the teacher has a proper assessment and evaluation of students achievement, his achievement becomes meaningless. Evaluation process helps a student to improve his achievement. Thus, "Evaluation signifies a wider, more comprehensive and continuous process of assessing student progress. It is integrated with the whole task of education and its purpose is to improve instruction and not merely to measure its achievement. In its highest sense, evaluation brings out the factors that are inherent in student growth such as proper attitudes and understanding."

Evaluation and Examination

There is distinction between evaluation and examination. Examination is less comprehensive than evaluation. A new technical term evaluation connotes a comprehensive concept of measurement. To quote J. W Wrightstone, "Evaluation is a relatively- new technical term introduced to designate a more comprehensive concept of measurement than is applied in conventional tests and examinations .... The emphasis in measurement is upon single aspects of subject-matter achievement or specific skills and abilities . The emphasis in evaluation is upon broad personality changes and major objectives of an educational programme. This includes not only the subject-matter achievement but also attitudes, interests, ideals, ways of thinking, work habits and personal and social abilities." Thus, evaluation helps the improvement of the achievement as well as the improvement of different traits of personality.

Objectives of Evaluation in Civics

(1) To assess the success of the educational system or the method of teaching.

(2) To find out the difficulties, limitations and achievements of the educands.

(3) To provide educational and vocational guidance and counselling.

(4) To examine the utility of the techniques and aids of the teaching.

(5) To find out the aptitude and the inclination of the student.

(6) To find out the basis for the classification of the students.

(7) To lay down the standards of life.

(8) To encourage the process of learning.

(9) To judge the success and efficiency of the teacher.

(10) To bring about reforms in the teaching and the curriculum.

Forms of Evaluation or Examination

The word 'examination' has been derived from the term 'examen' which means 'tongue of a balance'. The main object of examination is to have proper assessment of the work and the achievement of the students. This can be carried out by the teachers themselves 'or some outside agencies. Following are the forms or the methods of evaluation of examination.

(1) Observation technique

(2) Test technique

Observation technique: In observation technique of civics evaluation the behaviour, the activities and the aptitudes of the student are observed and examined in an organised and scientific manner.

Test technique: In test technique the teacher tries to find out about the knowledge of the students. He tries to judge their attainment and the achievement. Test technique has several forms, important amongst which are the following :

(i) Oral test

(ii) Practical test

(iii) Written test.

Oral test: It is essentially a personal test in which the student is made to furnish answer to certain questions, that are put to him orally. In oral test there is an interview of the educand by the examiner through which it is possible to find out the personal traits of the student, such as self-confidence, personal control, the method of speech, etc.

Practical test: In this method the student presents a project or a specimen of the work done by him.

Written test: In written test the student has to write out answers to certain questions within a prescribed limit of time. Following are the main forms of the written test :

(a) Traditional or essay type test

(b) Dissertation type test

(c) Objective or new type test.

Traditional or essay type test: This system of examination is very much in vogue in India. It is possible to test the power of expression, writing, style, language, etc., of the educand through this method. This system is, however, dominated by the subjective element. Therefore, it has been very much criticized. The need for examination reforms has been called for because of the defects of this essay type of test.

Dissertation type test: In this type of examination the examinee carries out research work on a prescribed topic and presents a dissertation that contains the results of the work done by him. The plan of this work is submitted in writing. It is an enlarged form of essay type test.

Objective or new type test: In order to meet the objections raised against the essay type test or the traditional examination system, a new system has been introduced known as 'Objective Test' or the 'New Type Test'. In this method, an attempt is made to judge the aptitude, intellect, inclination and the power of the judgement of the student. This type of examination is said to be free from the subjective element. It is capable of helping the teachers to have a proper idea of the attainment of the student.

Forms of the Objective Type of Test

***Recognition type test*:** An attempt is made to assess the power of recognition of the student through this method. The student has to find out the correct answer out of several answers given. There are the following sub-forms of this type of test :

(i) Alternate response type or true-false test

(ii) Multiple choice test

(iii) Matching type test

(iv) Classification type test

(v) Recall type test.

Alternate response type or true-false test: In this type of test, the answer is limited to the possibilities of true and false of the two or more alternatives given and the examinee has to choose one. Sometimes the signs of 'r' and 'x' are also required to be used.

Example of the Response Type or True-false Test

Given below are certain statements. Put the letter 'R' against the statements that are correct and 'W' against the statements that are wrong.

(a) Pakistan invaded Kargil in 98.

(b) Dr. K. R. Narayanan is the Prime Minister of India.

(c) The Prime Minister of India is elected by the people directly.

(d) Mr. Kalyan Singh is the Chief Minister of Uttar Pradesh.

Multiple choice type test: In this type of test, several answers are given to a particular question. The student is asked to find out the correct answer.

Example

Given below are several answers to a particular question. Put the sign of (Tick) against the correct answer.

(a) India secured freedom on January 26, 1948/August 15, 1947/ January 26, 1950.

(b) Mrs. Vijay Laxmi Pandit/Mrs. Sucheta Kripalani/Mrs. Indira Gandhi/Mrs. Tarkeshwari Sinha was the Prime Minister of India.

(iii) Matching test- In this type of test, the examinee is provided with two lists in which the subjects are not given in a serially ordered manner. The student is expected to serialize them and put them against each other. For example :

1. Dr. K. R. Narayanan	Prime Minister of India
2. Sri. A. B. Vajpayee	President of India
3. Yashwant Singh	Defence Minister of India
4. George Fernandes	Finance Minister of India.

Classification type test: In this type of test, the student is given a group of certain words. Out of these words, generally one word is irrelevant. The student is asked to underline that word. For example

Underline the word that is irrelevant.

Uttar Pradesh /Punjab/Haryana/Maharashtra/Calcutta/Kashmir/ Orissa.

Recall type test: In this type of test, the power of recall of the student is judged. He is asked to answer the questions that test his recall power. Following are the various types of recall type test

(i) Simple Recall type test; and

(ii) Completion test.

Simple Recall type test: In this type of test, the students are expected to answer the question on the basis of their memory. Given below is an example of this test

(a) When did India become a Republic?

(b) Who was the first Education Minister of India?

(c) When did Sri Jawahar Lal Nehru die?

Completion test: In this type of test, the examinees are given incomplete sentences. They are supposed to complete the sentences filling in proper words in the blank places. Given below is an example :

(1) The Prime Minister of India is the leader of the .... Party in Parliament.

(2) The members of Lok Sabha receive a monthly allowance of Rs.........

Evaluation or Examination

A question is often asked whether the examination system or the evaluation technique should be applied to the teaching of Civics as well, so that the achievement of the students may be judged. Generally it is believed that the written type of test or the essay type of examination is the correct method for assessing the achievement of the students. This is not wholly correct. As Civics involves a lot of practical knowledge, it is necessary to apply some sort of practical examination to judge the attainment of the students. The students should be given an opportunity to take part in collective activities, organise mock parliaments, courts, assemblies and councils, etc. They should be given an opportunity to learn the art of proper exercise of their franchise. They should be given responsible positions in games and other activities. This would provide them with an opportunity for acquiring the traits of leadership. While the students are provided with these types of opportunities, the teacher should continue to guide them properly.

With the help of the objective type of test students should also be given an opportunity to prove their power of recognition and recall.

Thus, though there is every place for evaluation and examination in Civics, a proper and scientific handling of the evaluation technique is needed. Through evaluation, it is possible to ascertain the knowledge of the examinees about the subject matter of civics.

Present System of Examination

Under the present system of examinations in this country, all the students are put in a single hall, at the end of each session, and answer books are distributed to each of them. At the appointed time, the question papers are distributed to them, following which during the space of two or three hours the student is expected to answer a required number of questions. Finally, the answer books are gathered and sent to an examiner whose appointment in that capacity is previously confirmed. Sometimes, the examiner is other than the person who sets the examination paper. If the student's attempt in the answer -books is considered worthy of being awarded 33 per cent marks by the examiner, he is deemed to have passed the said examination. If he fails to secure these marks, in the eyes of examiner, he is deemed to have failed to pass the examination. The individual who does not succeed is compelled to spend another session in the same class.

Defects of the Examination System

There is hardly any need to point out that the existing examination system is not conducive to the proper development of children. The following are some of its shortcomings that have been time and again pointed out by various educationists and commissions appointed for the purpose.

Students do not study throughout the whole year: For the present examination system, the student is not compelled to exert himself through the entire session, but achieves competency for it by labouring only through the last few weeks before the examination. In this manner, the student does not attain any real ability or capability even though he passes the examination. He forgets a lesson just as soon or as rapidly as he learns it. During the first two or three months of the session, it is a rare student who is seen at his desk. In this manner, from the educational viewpoint, a major portion of a student's time is totally wasted.

Studying from question-answer books and key books: In the present context, a student's ability is gauged from the scores he obtains in the examinations. And for obtaining good marks in the examinations, there is no need to wander into a maze of extensive reading and comprehensive knowledge. In every examination paper, the student is required to do four to six questions out of ten or twelve that are set. The consequence is that even without having gone through more than one-third of the course prescribed for study, the average student finds three or four questions that he is in a position to answer. And four to ten pages of writing are considered adequate in answer to each question. Thus, why should the student bother himself with reading bulky books that are likely to cause him untold misery and confusion? And the best books do not even include any clue as to the precise answer that would suit a particular question which is likely to be asked in the examination. Often, most of the students write out the answers to questions asked in previous years in the examinations for which they are preparing. This is considered one of the best methods of preparation for examination. And if the student discovers a book in the market that provides answers to all examination questions, then where is the need to write out these answers himself? Hence, the student instead of bothering to burden his brain with the actual text-books, studies from help books and succeeds in the examination. The books in question-answer form are not sufficiently brief so that the student desirous of further economising upon the effort to be expended in the examination can turn to a perusal of guess papers which include answers to possible examination questions in a total of approximately fifty to sixty pages. If the guess work turns out to be exact or if the student is lucky, he is sure to pass the examination. It is only too painfully evident that the student who passes his examinations in this manner possesses no knowledge whatsoever of his subject and the object of examination is as far as possible from being fulfilled.

Fear of examination: In the modern examination system the examination is taken at the end of the session with the result that the student is fearfully conscious of the examination right through the session. Teachers and students alike are normally engaged in the study of text-books, there being little or no time for the student to engage in the study and perusal of any general books, not directly pertaining to his curriculum. He is also in no position to develop any real interest in other things. The natural result is that the student is not aware of anything outside the course that is prescribed. And, no curriculum or book, can ever provide complete knowledge of any subject. For such comprehensive knowledge, it is essential that many books be studied and that this study be supplemented with the necessary experience of actual practical life. Under the present examination system, the fear of examination does not conduce to any extensive study.

Success in examinations a matter of luck: In the way examinations are conducted at present, success is more a matter of luck than of anything else. His entire future is to be decided in two or three hours. No matter what skill a student has gained in his subject through constant labour during the entire session, his effort is completely wasted if for some reason or the other he fails to exhibit his skill in these three hours. Some students fail to attend the examination through some contingency such as illness during the examination period, or an accident or any other human involvement. On the other hand, even though they are in a position to attend the examination, they fail to give their best performance. The only consequence, in such a case, is that their whole year's effort is wasted.

Mechanical method: In this way, the existing system of education is a machine in which conclusions are reached, while no importance being attached- to the human elements involved. Hence, people have devised new methods of succeeding in this mechanical set-up. Some students do not bother to put in more than a few weeks efforts for the examinations, during which they do nothing more than make a cursory study of guess papers and question-answer forms. As a result, they are in a position to come to grips with the paper, even though there is no element of mastery involved. And in subjects in which the question paper outdoes expectation, and unexpected questions crop up, the contingency is overcome by fraternizing with the examiners and having their marks surreptitiously increased. And in the case of such a success in any examination, it is only natural for the individual to be devoid of any skill whatsoever in the subject in which he has passed the examination.

Defects concerning evaluation of answer books: Under the present system of examination, a student's achievement in any subject is measured by the marks that he obtains during the examination. Hence, his fortune depends upon the fair evaluation of his effort in the answer book. Such a method is susceptible to numerous faults, some of them being enumerated below :

(i) If the teacher's mental condition is disturbed he does not evaluate the answer books correctly. What most often occurs is that the first copies in the bundle sent to him are examined with due care, but as he gradually tires and reaches a stage of growing exhaustion, the subsequent copies are gone through as a matter of necessity and duty.

(ii) It is only too apparent that all copies are not examined from the same standpoint or standard. Of course, different examiners would award differing marks to the same copy, but even if the same examiner is asked to examine the same copy, it is quite likely that he will award it different marks on different occasions.

(iii) The maximum number of marks that any student may be awarded depends upon the examiner's mental tendency. It is a common case that the subject in which the examiner himself has never managed to score more than 60% marks in any examination that he has taken, is one in which no student will ever be awarded high marks by such an individual since he is convinced that none is equal to him, let alone anyone being superior to him. On the other hand, other examiners are very liberal and are even capable of awarding marks upto 90%. If all the answer books of a particular subject were to go to one and the same examiner, there would be some saving grace, but it usually happens that the number of students studying a subject runs into thousands so that the examiners of it are also numerous. If an individual's copy falls into the hands of strict examiner, he is not likely to score well at all, while a less deserving candidate may score better than him if the latter's copy happens to have gone to a very liberal person. And this seems to be playing with the children's or student's career and capacities.

(iv) It often happens, that due to a very great variety of causes, the examiner has very little time at his disposal to examine the copies. One of the causes in such a case is the delayed arrival of the answer books themselves, but more often it is a case of the examiner's being busy or just careless. One natural outcome of such practice is that the teachers pay half their fee to have the answer books examined by other less qualified and in some cases completely unqualified individuals. Some teachers are so lacking in ethical sense that they have their wives and students do the work of examining the copies, even though they cannot be imagined to be qualified for the work. It is easy to understand the extent to which some innocent students suffer as the result of such behaviour on the part of teachers.

(v) Many of the examiners are completely prejudiced or biased in their thinking, having only the most incomplete knowledge of their respective subjects. Secondly, some teachers even fail to understand the actual implications of the questions asked in the question paper. It is only to be expected in such circumstances that there is no justice done to the student.

Long examination period: The present examination system allows the period of examination to spread over the very considerable period of at least a month. It is often seen that students get some two weeks between two individual examination dates. Such a long period of inactivity has the worst effect upon the student's attitude towards the examination as it tends to lull him towards the seriousness of the matter. Secondly, the provision of time periods between various papers is not at all proportionate. He gets no more than a few hours between two papers while between another two he has a few days at his disposal. Evidently, the opportunity available for the preparation of each subject is unequal.

Wrong objective: The present aim of examination is to obtain marks in order to get 'a degree, not the desire, to gain skill in any subject. Hence, the main attention in any examination is concentrated upon getting good marks so that one can have proof of one's ability or skill. There are many methods of obtaining an adequate number of marks in the examination, though all of them are not formal. One of the simplest is obtaining a certificate of success in an examination without actually appearing in it, irrespective of the fact that discovery of such an incriminating fact leaves them open to criminal action in a court of law. And the objective behind obtaining a certificate or degree is no more than securing a remunerative position that offers financial security in life. Thus, students who are not particularly desirous of securing a good status in life are often careless of studying hard to obtain a degree since they require no such passport to the good things of life. As a result of the contaminated and one-sided objectives of education existing at present, the system is riddled with defects and an inherent and chronic corruption.

Defects of the essay system: Under the existing scheme of examination, the student is required to answer each question in the form of an essay, with the result that the educational system has acquired all the defects inherent in the essay system. In this method, the students pay much greater attention to learning answers to question than to understanding the subject and delving deep into it. In the examination hall, they do no more than reproduce these well learned and remembered answers on the answer books. Once the examination is over, the facts learned for it are as expeditiously forgotten, since once they have been put in the answer book, they no longer possess any importance for the student. One natural outcome of this method is that even though the student may have done exceptionally well in the examination, he is more or less blank in all subjects that he has made a pretence of studying.

Suggestions for Improving the Examination System

Many thinkers, educationists and education commissions have pointed out the above defects in the existing scheme of examinations in this country, but there are many difficulties that hinder the complete replacement of it. The main difficulty is financial besides which the extremely large number of candidates make it difficult to evolve a different examination system for them. Hence, the practicable solution is to maintain the existing scheme of things and make efforts to effect definite improvements. Main suggestions in this respect are the following :

Certificates should not be required for services: If the tradition of requiring certificates for various jobs and services is given up, and the individuals are separately tested for qualities that the job requires, then people will give up the race for obtaining certificates and degrees, and turn their attention to developing qualities required in the professions of their choice. It must, of course, be kept in mind that this method is not practicable in all professions, nevertheless, it should be used in as many as admit of its use.

Improvement in the evaluation of answer books: The method and system of examining and evaluating answer books should be improved. The remuneration of evaluating copies should be enough to induce the examiner to attend to them himself, and to do this work efficiently and well. The time allowed to the examiner for evaluating the answer books should be sufficient to allow him to work in peace so that no haphazard work results from hurry or strain. There should be a definite standard of references concerning the answer of different questions. Every examiner should be required to send copies that he has examined as samples so that his standard of judgement can be measured, and he should be requested to evaluate the remaining copies similarly.

Terminal or monthly examinations: Nevertheless, the student's knowledge of his subject cannot be properly gauged once in a year in a sitting of only three hours. For this it is essential that the teacher should examine the students in the class every fifteen days or a month in the subject matter that he has taught till then. The results should be announced on the basis of these monthly tests as well as the annual examination. This method will compel the students to spread their labour over the whole year.

Examination in other aspects of development: The aim of education is not only to impart information but to achieve the complete development of the individual. It is only information that is examined in the present examinations. Hence, it is essential that the child's physical, emotional and social development also be examined, even though the marks obtained therein may not be made the reason for detaining him if he fails. Yet, these marks will help in advising and improving him. If the children understand that it is essential for them to pass in these respects also they themselves will try harder to improve themselves.

Re-examination of those who fail to attend regular examinations: Examinees, who, for one or the other legitimate reason such as disease, accident, etc., fail to attend their examination at the regular time, should be given a chance to be examined once the reason for their abstaining from the regular examination has been confirmed. Their efforts during the entire year should not be allowed to go waste.

Discouragement to rote learning: Questions in the examination papers should be such as discourage the practice of rote learning but encourage the expression of the student's skill in the subject. Questions should vary radically from year to year so that the practice of basing preparation and guess papers on questions asked in previous years and then rote learning answers to them is discouraged and ultimately discarded.

Wide range of question papers: Questions in 'the examination paper should cover every aspect of the curriculum even if more than one questions are given, and the solution of one is required. Such methods will induce the students to study all that is prescribed rather than making a selection from it.

Equitable distribution of examination period: During the period of examinations, the distribution of papers should be equitable and proportionate, the normal period of inactivity not stretching over more than one or two days. Only one paper should be set for one day.

Increase in the number of examiners: The number of examiners should be considerably increased so that all of them can conveniently judge a smaller number of copies in the period of one or two weeks provided to them for the purpose.

Punishment for corrupt practices: Strict measures should be adopted for punishing all examiners who resort to corrupt measures in passing examinations or obtaining certificates.

Finally, the fundamental fact that must be pointed out is that the improvement in the existing scheme of examination depends upon the teachers themselves. It is for them to encourage the students in their classes to attain high degree of skill and efficiency in the subject rather than to prepare them for the examinations. In educational institutions, the principal teacher can specially attend to this aspect of the matter. Cooperation between teachers and the various examining bodies can help to improve the system of examinations.

QUESTIONS

1. Giving the meaning and purpose of evaluation, throw light on the importance of evaluation in Civics.
2. Discuss the importance of evaluation in Civics.
3. How does a new type attainment test differ from traditional test? Illustrate your answer with two types framed on Civics syllabus prescribed for any stage of school course?
4. What are the defects of the existing system of examination? Give your suggestions for its improvement?

10
Role of the Teacher

Education is a tri-polar process. At one end, there is the educand, at the other the subject-matter and at the third end is the teacher. Teacher is the real source of education, though the child is the focal point around which the whole process of education revolves. Subject-matter and the teacher are secondary to the child. The teacher tries to teach the subject-matter to the child. While teaching the child, he has to keep an eye on his psychological requirements.

Prof. Bining has rightly said: "Teacher is the pivot around which the whole educational system moves." The teacher play an important role in the process of education. He handles the subject-matter in order to equip the student for the future life. On account of this role the teacher is called the builder of the nation. If a country has a team of successful teachers, the nation progresses by leaps and bounds. If a nation has incompetent teachers, it is sure to go down.

Importance of the Teacher

The teacher of Civics has an added value and importance in a democratic set up. He trains the students for ideal citizenship. A democracy can run successfully- only if it has conscious citizens. It is the teacher who develops these qualities in the students. He is like a gardener who tends the tender plants of the society and helps them to blossom forth into full bloom and fragrance. In this regard, teacher of civics tries to fill the fragrance of ideal citizenship into the future flowers of the land.

Duties of the Teacher

The main job of the Civics teacher is to inculcate the values of ideal citizenship in the students. In order to achieve this objective he has to undertake the following :

Be a student of students: The civics teacher has to act as a student of the students. He has to study the interests, aptitudes and other mental faculties of the students and with an eye on all these mental faculties impart knowledge of civics to them.

Keep up to date: Civics teacher has to keep himself up-to-date about the problems of civic life. He should know the most recent events of the civic life.

Curriculum construction: No curriculum of Civics can be complete and up-do-date as Civics is an ever growing subject. To act as a Curriculum Construction Expert the teacher of Civics has to fit in the various developments of the civic life in the curriculum in such a way that the students may find it to be of interest and value to them.

To act as link: The most important task of a Civics Teacher is to act as a link between the School and the civic life at large. He should establish correlationship between the social life and the school and the life of various other associations and social groups. As the main aim of civics teaching is to establish an ideal civic life, it is the duty of the Civics Teacher to encourage the students to play their role in this direction.

Traits of a Successful Teacher

To discharge the tasks expected from him a Civics Teacher should have the following traits in him :

(1) Traits of an ideal citizen

(2) Faith in the teaching of the subject and profession

(3) Thorough knowledge of Civics and related subjects

(4) Impartiality and scientific outlook

(5) Sympathy and creative imagination

(6) Impressive and interesting personality

(7) Faith in democracy

(8) Love and affection for the students

(9) Ideal social worker

(10) Ideal leader,

(11) Properly equipped with knowledge and character.

Traits of ideal citizen: As example is always better than a precept, the civics teacher has to prove his sayings all the more by his actions. In practical aspect, civics has to train young students to become ideal citizens. A Civics teacher has to present the example of ideal citizenship to be able to encourage the students to acquire the traits of ideal citizenship.

Faith in the teaching of the subject and the profession: Unless a person has faith in the job that he is entrusted, he will not be able to do full justice to it. This faith encourages a person to acquire more and discharge his duties in an ideal manner. The Civics teacher should have faith in the profession as well as the utility of teaching Civics to the students.

Unless the teacher is convinced of the utility of teaching Civics, he shall not be able to do justice to the subject.

Thorough knowledge of civics and related subjects: The civics teacher should have a thorough knowledge of civics subjects. Unless he has command over civics he shall not be able to present the subject matter before the students in an interesting manner. He should also know the correlationship of Civics with other social sciences. He should also be aware of the current events and the duties of a citizen. He should know where the interest of the nation lies. Unless he has all this knowledge he shall not be able to teach the students successfully.

Impartiality and scientific outlook: The Civics teacher should be impartial. He should try to present the subject-matter in an objective manner. Unless he is able to do that, he shall not be able to inculcate the spirit of true citizenship in the students. If he colours the subject-matter with his personal views, likes and dislikes, he shall not be doing justice to the students and the subject.

His presentation of the subject-matter of civics should be systematic and proper. This is possible only when the civics teacher has a scientific outlook.

***Sympathy and creative imagination*:** The emotion of sympathy enables a teacher to understand students' difficulties properly. It also helps him to know the viewpoints of the students. Creative imagination helps him to present the civics subject-matter in a lively and interesting manner. Ross has rightly remarked that the person from whom a gift of sympathy is withheld should not be a teacher.

***Impressive and interesting personality*:** Personality of the teacher plays an important role in the class room. If the teacher has an impressive and interesting personality he is able to impress the students well. It is quite possible that a teacher may have certain drawbacks in the personality but he can overcome them by certain other accomplishments.

***Faith in democracy*:** Citizenship is very much required for a democratic way of life. Unless the teacher has full faith in democracy and democratic way of life, it shall not be possible for him to teach civics properly. For efficient functioning of democracy the citizens must know their rights and obligations. They have to be conscious of their social obligations and requirements. Only such teacher, who has full faith in democracy, can teach all these things to his students.

***Love and affection for the students*:** The teacher of Civics should be master of child psychology and educational psychology. Unless he has the knowledge of all these things as well as the knowledge of the method of teaching and the principles and objectives of teaching, he cannot discharge his job successfully. The teacher who is endowed with all these qualities, shall have love and affection for his students. He should treat the students as if they were his own kith and kin and would treat them sympathetically. Such an atmosphere is congenial for teaching, specially for the teaching of Civics.

Ideal social worker: The teacher of Civics tries to build the lives of his students. This life building can be possible only when he is intimate with the spirit of social service. Developing the students into ideal citizens is the greatest social service that can be done. The teaching of Civics has a practical aspect in this regard. The teacher of Civics should act as a social worker and inculcate in the students the spirit of social service and ideal citizenship.

Ideal leader: The teacher of Civics should have the qualities of an ideal leader. A teacher who has this quality is able to impress the students more. He is able to guide the students in the proper direction. Since teaching of Civics has the practical aspect as well, an ideal leader can lead his followers in the right direction.

Properly equipped: The teacher of Civics should be properly equipped. He should know the method of teaching as well as other requirements of a teacher. As already stated he should have the knowledge of child psychology as well as educational psychology. If he has these qualities he will be able to do a real job. Prof. Hardikar has summed up these qualities in the following words :

"A teacher of Civics must be, in short, himself a good and worthy citizen, like an American citizen in the days of Pericles. Only a citizen teacher can induce civic consciousness in his pupils."

Teacher's Training

Civics teaching is not something that anybody can do without any kind of training. For efficient civics teaching it is necessary that the educator must have education of the highest level accompanied by training in techniques of teaching, principles of teaching, solution of educational problems, curriculum, organization of the school, etc. Different kinds of training is required for teaching at the different levels of education, and with this end in view, the kind and nature of training required for teaching at the primary, secondary and higher levels of education, have been determined. In ancient India the educand learn' the art of teaching from his own teacher without going to any independent teacher training establishment. The problems of training teachers arose when the British government in India set up a department of education to look after the educational needs of the country.

Kinds of Teacher Training

Different levels of training are required for teaching educands at different levels of education, and for this purpose different institutions are required. In India teachers concerned with teaching at the primary level and middle schools, are trained at normal training schools. Teachers for the high school level are trained in training colleges. In the universities, the B.Ed. and M.Ed. classes are intended to train individuals for teaching and functioning as principals in high schools and intermediate colleges. In addition to this, the country also has various institutions for providing special training in the teaching of home science, art, physical education, etc. But in view of the growing demand for trained teachers in all these spheres, one is obliged to say that the provisions for teacher's training in the country are wholly inadequate.

Problems of Training

The following is a brief account of the difficulties facing the training of teachers in the country :

***Absence of any coordination between school and training schools*:** In India, the training that is imparted to the trainee in the teacher's training schools bears little relation to the kind of teaching actually required in the schools, and hence this training does little to prepare him practically for teaching. K.G. Saiyeden has pointed out that instead of the theories learnt by the trainee and his actual conduct in the classroom, becoming synthesized and complementing to each other, they have in fact become two separate and disconnected facts.

***Absence of a balance between theory and practice*:** It is desirable that there should be a balance between principles and practices taught in the training colleges. In actual fact, training in most centres is concentrated on theoretical teaching without providing adequate opportunity for putting these theories into practice and thus testing them.

Defective curriculum: What is really desirable is that training colleges should teach only those subjects which are required for teaching in the schools, but in actual fact it is found that this basic principle is never in mind in determining the curriculum of the training college. As a consequence, the trainee studies many subjects which he is never required to teach.

Absence of freedom: In most training colleges, the trainees have little freedom to develop their independent personality. Their only immediate concern is to pass the examination somehow and to obtain their certificate of merit.

Neglect of human values: Little or nothing is done in the course of day to day training during the session to make the trainee aware of the ideals guiding human behaviour. K.G Saiyeden has pointed out that when the attention is centred on minor details and technical necessities due to narrow mindedness, all views of the relation between the school and society and the awareness of the actual problems of living are lost sight of.

Defective selection: As a general rule one finds that the number of applicants for admission to such colleges is far in excess of the sets or accommodation available. As a result the individuals selected are chosen for reasons other than their merits. Very often, no less than half the trainees in the B.Ed. classes are selected on recommendation and personal contact. As a result, many very able individuals are deprived of training.

Problems of in-course training: The problems besetting the in-course training through refresher courses, short-term courses, committees, summer institutes, are different in nature, inasmuch as they centre around the curriculum, selection, difference in theory and practice, etc.

Suggestions for Improvement

Educationists and education commissions have frequently pointed out the need to improve the attractiveness of education as a profession. Dr. S. Radhakrishnan said that the teacher has an important place in society, for it is his lot to transmit intellectual tradition from one generation to the next, to maintain technical efficiency and to prevent the torch of culture from burning out. He guides not only the individuals but the entire nation. Drawing attention to the pitiable lot of teachers in the country, Dr. Sampurnanand, the former chief minister, and also education minister of U.P commented, "The nation must realize the difficulties and the feelings of the teachers who are expected to provide men of ability and character and leaders in every sphere of life while they themselves have to work under conditions not calculated to foster either efficiency or self-respect." The Kothari Commission for education suggested that better salaries must be paid to teachers at all levels of education. In addition to this, the commission also advanced the following suggestions for improving the lot of teachers :

(1) A model Act should be prepared to control appointment of teachers to the universities.

(2) The post of principal in the school should be held only by an educated individual.

(3) When the teacher's ability improves, he should be given higher salaries.

(4) In the universities, special additional posts should be created for scholars.

(5) After every five years, the pay scales and dearness allowances rates should be reconsidered according to the change in prices.

(6) A teachers welfare fund should be established, and the teachers themselves should be asked to contribute one and-a-half per cent of their income.

(7) Retirement benefit should be extended to every class of teacher.

(8) The age of superannuation should be 60 to 65 respectively in schools and colleges.

(9) Teachers should also be given travel concessions so that they can tour the country every five years or so.

(10) In order to give national recognition to brilliant teachers, the number of awards should be increased.

Despite the very concrete suggestions laid down by the Kothari Commission almost no active measures have been undertaken to improve the profession of teaching and render it more attractive. In many schools, even today the teacher is not paid a fixed salary, and appointments to most institutions are controlled by recommendations rather than merit. In many schools, the trained teachers are not given salaries according to grades determined by the Government. In many cases, the management committees have remarkable extensive powers to terminate the service of teachers, thus rendering the teacher completely insecure. There is little reason for a brilliant and qualified individual to come to education when he is faced with poverty and insecurity. Hence, it is necessary that the state and the people must cooperate to remove these difficulties.

QUESTIONS

1. What are the various qualities and characteristics of an ideal civics teacher? Discuss.
2. Describe the functions of Civics teacher and throw light on his chief qualities.
3. A teacher can 'foster the qualities of ideal citizenship'. Examine the statement and comment.
4. What should be the attitude of a Civics teacher? Write a short essay on the qualities of a successful Civics Teacher.

11
Utility of Textbooks

Most of the education was imparted orally and verbally before script came into existence and press came into being. This tradition was all the more prevalent in India. Text-books came to be used in education at a very late stage. In the western world, text-books came to be used in education after French Revolution. Later on this device was employed in America. In India the text-books were used after script came into existence and the verbal knowledge was transcribed on the leaves of the trees. In the Islamic world, Holy Quran, a written book, formed the text-book of the earliest education of the child.

Importance of Textbooks

Text-books are important in the field of education. They are a device of imparting knowledge to the students. They save a lot of time and economise on human labour. H.R. Douglus has rightly said "In the last analysis with the great majority of the teachers, the text-book is a potential determinant of what and how they will teach. The teacher is the workman who moulds the lives of the students into various forms. He has to use the text-books as the instruments. If the instruments are not good the workman shall not be able to present his best. Similarly if the text books are not good, the teacher is not able to present the best before the students." Raymont has rightly said: "The text book must be regarded as strictly subordinate and supplementary to the teacher's lessons." John Dewey and Mahatma Gandhi revolted against bookish knowledge. This led to the attempts made by some for dispensing with the requirements of textbooks as an instrument and tool for imparting knowledge. In the first half of the 20th century, a thorough testing was undertaken by some thoughtful students of education in the USA to experiment with the bookless or a nearly bookless system. They arrived at a conclusion that the text-book could not be dropped out of the system of education.

Integral Part of Education

Educationists in India as well as abroad agree that the text-book is an integral part of any education system. According to the report of the Text-book Committee of the Central Advisory Board of Education, "A Modern educational system without text-books is as difficult to imagine as Hamlet without the prince of Denmark." The position of text-books in the educational system of U.S.A. has been summed up in these words: "Although text-books are considered only one of many instructional resources, the fact remains that many teachers are generally dependent on them... Generally speaking, text-books play a more prominent role in high school instruction than in the elementary grades. In some schools, the course of study for a given subject is still determined by the contents of text-books."

Thus, the text-book constitutes an inseparable part of any system of education today. Even in the most developed countries, where a variety of teaching-learning tools and techniques are available in the class-rooms, text-books continue to enjoy their rightful place. In a developing country like India where even the minimum essential requirements of a class-room are hardly provided, the need for quality text-books cannot be over-emphasised.

As far as civics is concerned, the text-book is an indispensable aid to all methods of study. In school work in civics the text-book remains after the teacher, the learners' chief aid support. A well-chosen text-book is a useful adjunct to the efforts of the teacher and a reassurance to the pupil.

In the USA, text-books are used in civics from the earliest classes, but in European schools, civics text-books are rarely in use in primary classes. In Indian schools, text-books are in use from the earliest to the highest classes and all civics lessons are based on text-books.

Indispensable in Teaching

Good text-books are indispensable for the study and teaching of civics for the following reasons.

Helping the teacher: It provides useful guidelines along which the teacher who can plan his day-to-day teaching; text-book serves as a reference book. While actually teaching in the class-rooms; text book provides suggestions for some assignments; and activities to be taken up in the class-room and outside. Text book can, thus, be a constant standby of the civics teacher: It can be used to aid the teacher who has run out of new ideas.

Helping the pupil: A text-book is the most accessible guide for the pupil, a dependable reference book and an all-time companion. The pupil makes use of it to prepare himself in advancement 'of learning in the class-room. He refers to it during the course of learning in the classroom. He revises and reinforces the class-room learning. He does assignments at home; prepares for the examination; reads for pleasure; and seeks guidance and reference for further studies from the text books.

Providing minimum essential knowledge at one place: A text-book is a constant standby of the civics teacher, as it gives the minimum knowledge at one place. Some mature, well-trained, experienced teachers may find it possible to use their outlines and thus may dispense with a basal text-book, but most teachers cannot and should not do it.

Self-teaching: The tradition of imparting education through lecturing has high value when the teacher is armed with special gifts of inspiring of the gifted and encouraging the weak students, etc. But even the impact of best spoken messages is necessarily transitory in character, even the most attentive listener loses any but the obvious connection in the lesson. The efficacy of the text-book lies in making self-teaching a possible proposition through printed materials. *A* good text-book is insurance against illiteracy at home normal in the case of many Indian children.

Providing logical and comprehensive material: A good text-book provides material in a systematic and comprehensive form. It sets a standard of minimum essential to be achieved by pupils of all categories. It gives the beginner a grasp of new matter. It gives direction for further studies to enthusiastic pupils.

Ensuring uniformity of a good standard: A text-book provides a highway for carrying better practices to all schools. It ensures some sort of uniformity of good standard. It furnishes a common basis to master the process of reading, analysing, outlining and summarising. It furnishes a common laboratory to develop study skills.

Providing a base from which both the teacher and the pupils may start and continue to work: Containing the minimum essential knowledge the text-book provides a point of departure for a mere comprehensive link. It provides the common ground which both the students and teachers may explore together. It focuses attention on the same issues- events, sequences and circumstances and serves as a rallying point.

Providing both confirmation and sustenance: A text-book is supposed to contain the facts carefully sifted and examined. It confirms the knowledge obtained elsewhere. "When preparing his famous lectures on modern history even Lord Acton was found writing with a pedestrian text-book of European history at his elbow to ensure presumably that inspiration did not lead him beyond the bounds of recorded facts."

Rectifing the limitations of the class-room situation in most of the Indian schools: Following limitations of class-room situations in India warrant the use of civics text-books :

(i) A large number of students in each class, creating congestion.

(ii) Lengthy courses and teachers' worries about finishing the prescribed syllabus within the specified period.

(iii) Extremely divergent opinions regarding historical, political and social events.

(iv) Non-availability of other teaching aids and devices indispensable for effective instruction.

Ensuring intellectual rapprochement of peoples: Civics text-books can coordinate the activities and bring about the intellectual rapprochement of people. They can serve as organs of national co-ordination.

A single text-book may become a crutch, a burdensome milestone round the neck, a limited view or a tedious bore, but there is little doubt that many teachers find civics text-book the most useful tool in their repertoire.

What is a Textbook?

A text-book differs from an ordinary book mainly on the score that it combines within it teaching-learning techniques and motives. It is a specially written book which contains selective and systematic knowledge. In it every care is taken for coherence and sequence. It is made simple to the degree that suits the intended learner. It is not a bare statement of knowledge but armed with various teaching-learning devices to fulfil the desired instructional role. Its subject-matter receives a rich dose of pedagogy with all its implications, such as devices for practice, application, motivation and fixation of learning. That is why a text-book is said to be "the teacher in print."

Functions of the Textbooks

In the Junior classes: It can be relied on for essential information, so organised as to show order and continuity, and so presented as to be clear, interesting and attractive.

For the senior classes: It should contain a well-arranged comprehensive knowledge to enable them to prepare for their examination. It should expand its scope and size to meet the changing conception of what is considered educationally sound and desirable.

Criteria for a Good Textbook

As a text-book is only an aid or tool, it must contain all the qualifications of an aid or tool to be helpful and useful. A good civics text-book must satisfy the following criteria :

Achieving the purposes of teaching civics: A good text book should assume special responsibility towards the promotion of national goals like secularism and national integration. It should enable children to appreciate India's rich cultural heritage and to recognise and get rid of what is undesirable and antiquated. Through its content, style of presentation, exercises and illustrations, it should provide the understandings necessary for the promotion of national goals.

Child-centred: A good text-book on civics should be suitable to the age, ability and interest of pupils. It should be primarily addressed to pupils of a particular age group and of a particular society. As the world of the child expands in concentric circles as he grows, so his textbook must reflect the stage he has reached.

Fluent narration: Instead of a bare outline of a series of cut and dried facts a text should have both chatty, descriptive and brightly coloured details and a lot of explanation of why things happen. There should not only be, "what" of people and events but also "how", "why", "where", and "when" of them. It should not only give the result but also the long tedious and doubtful struggles that produced the results. In the words of Richard Livingstone, "There are no final moments in human affairs, no Armageddon, no decisive battle which settles everything. There is only a long campaign for a better world, lasting centuries and indeed millennia; and for such long campaigns we ought to have short-term objectives, but may have very long-term views." A text book should have details enough to lend colour and warmth. The facts should be clothed in proper flesh and blood so that the pupils may be interested in reading them. The young must go to a text book to find something. The old theory "small child, small book," does not hold good especially in relation to story of man's experiences.

Clear and self-explanatory arrangement: A good text book should have a detailed table of contents: with the material arranged under headings and sub-headings to be easily comprehended by the pupils.

Opening up various avenues of thought and study: Civics should never be something that comes out of a book. Civics text-book should make it evident that what is given in the book is only a beginning. It should create interest and help to develop that interest by suggestions as to how the matter given in the book may be followed up and developed. It should give references to other books on the same subject suited to the age of the pupils. It should widen their outlook, develop their interests and open new vistas of knowledge and discovery.

The language should be suitable for the "reading age' of the pupils: A text-book for the younger children should be especially written in simple sentences so as to establish an effective communication with them. The language used should be accurate and appropriate so that it helps in enriching children's language.

Well-illustrated: The abstract concepts presented in the text-book should be illustrated through visual aids, such as photographs, maps, time-lines, pictures, picture-diagrams, etc. The text book should be attractive, inviting, a pleasure to look at and read. Illustrations should be well chosen and connected with the main theme. As young children like colours, coloured illustrations have an important place in civics text-books for primary classes. The size of the illustration should be such that the children may easily make out the various details. The illustration should be meaningful for the children.

Illustrations explain the text or supplement and complement the text. Therefore, constant reference to the illustrations in the text is very essential. A good civics text-book helps the children to make maximum use of illustrations by giving captions, explanatory notes and exploratory questions along with the illustrations. Illustrations given in the text-book of civics must be very accurate and realistic.

Simple, interesting and attractive to be a self-study reader: Pupils should be able to take advantage of the civics text-book with the least help from the teacher and parents. It should give exercises at the end of a unit/topic to enable the pupils to focus their attention on the right points in the discussion for concentrated study. It should help them to know whether they have gained what is expected from the study of a topic. It may contain such instructions as:

(i) Answer the questions given below;

(ii) Locate the following places on appropriate maps;

(iii) Locate following dates on the appropriate time-line.

Free from indoctrination: A good civics text book should present a comparative view of the ideas of different people expressed on a particular phase of life. It should not contain superficial and misleading generalisations like "the Chinese are cruel and secretive", or "the Pakistanis are dangerous." It should not contain too much nationalism which tends to be dogmatic, conclusive and official. It should not sow the seeds of hasty reflexes, snap judgements, and emotional reactions. Biases, prejudices of writers should not reflect in text book. It should tell the truth, the whole truth and nothing but the truth.

Providing proper and adequate exercises and suggestions for activities, etc, at the end of each chapter: In a good text book exercises should flow from the main text, supplement and complement it, so that the following purposes are achieved :

(a) Helping pupils in recapitulating and revising the important information.

(b) Engaging pupils in practice which help in the better understanding of the various concepts and information.

(c) Involving pupils in activities as discussion and debates, preparation of time lines and maps, etc., which develop skills related to the chapter.

(d) Making pupils participate in activities which foster the desired habits, attitudes and behaviour patterns.

(e) Giving suggestions to gifted children of the class for challenging assignments.

(f) Helping the teacher in evaluating the children in terms of their acquisition of desired understandings, attitudes and skills.

Containing the lesson units framed by teachers for a particular topic: This enables the pupils to derive maximum benefit from a text-book. They find the text-book material meaningful and relevant.

Up-to-date: Civics is an area of the curriculum whose content, emphasis and treatment are undergoing modifications in the light of new researches, events and movements. Therefore, it is essential that the civics text-book is frequently revised to eliminate those things which no longer hold good and to add those which have to play a significant role. The text-book must contain the latest information, eliminating mistakes and stereotyped views. The sources from which the information is drawn should be authentic.

***Developing international understanding*:** A good Civics text-book should emphasise cultural relations between the nations of the world and the contribution of different nations to world civilisation.

Containing references for further study and references for collateral reading: This motivates the interested pupils to pursue their studies further.

Catering to the needs of backward pupils: This requires small but leading questions at the end of every sub-topic.

Promoting group effort: The civics text-book should contain suggestions for group projects with every topic. Assignments with divisions may be suggested which could be jointly attempted by the groups. It should contain suggestions on constructing models, preparing charts, etc.

Containing a subject index at the end: This is especially in a text-book for higher classes; index is given to develop independent study habits in pupils. It helps in forming a habit of making references and comparisons in pupils and facilitating a combination of topics with chronological approach.

Should there be a Single Prescribed Textbook?

Should a single text-book or more than one text-book be prescribed for civics teaching for a particular class. A single text-book is likely to constitute a boundary and set a limit. The pupils may develop a wrong idea that civics means the text-book of civics. However good the 'staple' text-book, it is unlikely to be good enough to act as the pupil's sole support. Therefore, the teacher should prescribe a single text-book as a standby and make available a set of text-books, each presenting subject-matter from a different point of view. This will minimise the tendency to depend solely on the printed word and the pupils will be able to compare and contrast different viewpoints.

Proper Use of Textbook

Giving definite information: As a store-house of basic information, text-book contains narrative details. The teacher may guide the pupils in knowing the essentials and through it how much he should remember.

Establishing common background of basic information on the part of all the pupils: The use of the text-book is helpful in introducing pupils to sum up the key ideas of the unit, acquaint them with the vocabulary and help them learn enough about the topic to be able to proceed intelligently.

Setting exercises: Civics text-book can be used for setting logical and imaginative exercises. The pupils may be asked to write answers to questions or they may be put to situations in which they are supposed to give their own imaginative answers. Exercises can be set for compiling the list of the things people would have used or needed in certain circumstances. Questions set on the illustrations given in the text-book may be a subject of serious attention.

These fix the information, help the pupils to think of events as having actually happened, and give them opportunity to use their imagination in transforming text-book information into something which, is personal and vivid.

Summarising learning: Civics text-book can be used to summarise the learning of the unit activities.

Point of departure: Civics text-book may serve as a point of departure for unit study, a frequent point of recall and a point of return.

When to Use Textbook?

If the teacher follows Civics text-books in teaching class lessons, it is easier for the pupils to follow the lesson and the text-book. If the teacher follows the text-book but presents the material in a novel manner adding interesting anecdotes, the approach is better. It is advisable that the lesson delivered by the teacher contains page references to text-book and other reference books. This would prevent the pupils from following the text-book slavishly. It would also help them to develop an independent approach to the study of civics text-book.

If the teacher asks the pupils to read a particular lesson from the text-book before he delivers the lesson it will pay rich dividends. To enable the pupils to become familiar with the new subject-matter they should be asked to read the lesson in advance. It will be easier for them to comprehend the material without much effort.

Opinions are divergent about the use of the text-book during the lesson. But there is unanimity on the point that the text-book should never be made a substitute for a class lesson. It should always be supported for a class-lesson. It should always be supported by class-lessons made interesting with the help of various devices as stories, illustrations, use of original sources, while the pupils may get details from the textbooks, reference books, etc. general ideas may be developed with the help of examples.

Civics text-book needs to be studied thoroughly. The questions may be given to the pupils which they should be asked to answer with the help of material given in the text and reference books.

Civics text-book may be used for setting objective type-questions for internal tests, to ensure that the pupils do read the text-book thoroughly and have a basic knowledge of civics.

Precautions in the Use of Textbook

Text-book to be subsidiary and supplementary: The text-book should be considered a means by which the student is helped in his study. He should never think that his task is simply to learn what is given in the book.

No Recitation of text book in the class: Recitation of the text-book in the class is a waste of time.. It may occasionally be useful to read aloud a passage of special importance.

Critical approach: The teacher should not be an uncritical mouthpiece for what is contained in the text-book. Like the best of human beings, the best of text-books are fallible. It should not become the whole outline, content and plan. It should not monopolise the whole time of the pupil. It should not become the sole source of reading. On the highest level, it may be used as a supplement, a basis for common understanding and a point of departure. It should not dominate or determinate the content or procedure of the courses.

The overall use of text-book should be to achieve the objectives of the teaching of civics. Attempts should be made to stimulate pupil's imagination to know more of civics and to rationalise cause effect relationship relating to different events. There should be well-graded and thought-provoking questions making the text-book means to realise desirable objectives. If used effectively civics text-book would vitalise instruction in the class and give a new meaning to teaching and learning.

Preparation of Textbooks

Preparation of civics text-books is a challenging job which may be taken up only by experienced teachers and learned scholars combining scholarship with experience, knowledge of schools and their needs.

Some writers believe that text books should be nationalised in the interests of national integration, others advocate that undue emphasis on national needs may result in dull uniformity. When the 10 + 2 + 3 pattern was introduced, text-books were prepared by Central Board of Secondary Education and NCERT Later, in the IX Conference of the Boards of Secondary Education held at Chandigarh from Feb. 10-12, 1978, it was decided that NCERT should concentrate on the production of instructional material and that State Governments, education/examinations boards, schools and other educational agencies, should be free to adapt and develop this material to suit their particular needs.

Utility of Textbooks in the Teaching

Civics is a part of social studies. Text-books should be used economically in the teaching of Civics. They should be used for helping the students to strengthen their experiences. They should help the students to revise the lesson learnt in the class room after going out of the school. They should also help the students to write down the answers of the question given by the teacher.

Civics text-books should serve as tools in the hands of the teachers. They should help the teachers to make their teaching more authentic, successful and effective. Earnest Horne has rightly remarked

"One of the most effective ways for improving the content and method of instruction is to place better text-books in the hands of teachers and pupils." To quote Prof. Hardikar "The text-book is a totality of items of knowledge, habits, feelings, activities and attitude."

Textbooks for Various Stages of Education

(1) Primary,

(2) Junior High School

(3) Secondary and

(4) Higher.

Textbooks for Primary classes: In primary classes the students up to the age of 11 come to receive education. They are very fond of listening to stories. Curiosity is their basic instinct. Text-books intended for this stage of education, should have the following traits in them:

(i) The subject-matter should be presented in the form of a story.

(ii) Books should be profusely illustrated with a good deal of charts and pictures.

(iii) To enable the students to understand the subject-matter easily and quickly they should be written in a simple language and lucid style.

(iv) They should be written with an eye on the psychological requirements of the children of this age.

(v) These books should not be very bulky.

(vi) The subject-matter of the book should be based on the principle of selectivity. Subject-matter useful for developing certain requisite qualities in the children of this age group should find a place in these text-books.

(vii) These books should be in accordance with the syllabus and the curriculum laid down for this stage of education.

(viii) The title cover of the book should be very attractive so that it may catch the eyes of students at the first glance.

(ix) Books should be reasonably priced. Their cost should not be beyond the reach of the common man.

(x) The text book should inculcate social qualities in the students.

(xi) As the main aim of teaching Civics is to produce ideal citizens of the country, it should be developed at this stage of education with the help of these text-books.

(xii) Activity and creativity should be developed in the students with the help of these text-books. The subject-matter should be so presented that there may be a good deal of scope for creative activities in the students.

Textbooks for Junior High School classes: Students between the age group of 11 and 14 are found at this stage of education. These are on the gateway of adolescence. They do not take interest in listening to stories only they want to face the realities of life. Intended for the students of this stage of education textbooks of civics should be written in a narrative style. In order to be useful, they should have the following traits

(i) They should be written with an eye on the mental and the physical age of the students.

(ii) They should keep in view the interest, aptitudes and talents of the student.

(iii) The subject-matter should be properly graded.

(iv) There should be certain questions for recapitulation at the end of each chapter.

(v) Their printing and get up should be flawless and attractive.

(vi) There should be attractive, precise and neatly drawn charts, pictures, illustrations, etc.

(vii) The text-books should meet the aims and objectives of the teaching of Civics at this stage of education.

(viii) They should develop the qualities of ideal citizenship in the students.

(ix) An attempt should be made to develop the social qualities in the students.

(x) Civics is a subject which requires more of practical training than theoretical teaching. This training has to begin at the Junior High School stage of education. Text-books should aim at this objective.

Textbooks for Secondary classes: This is the stage of adolescence. Students between 14-18 years of age come and receive education at this level. Students are interested in taking a practical view of life. They want to solve problems by themselves. They have no more interest in listening to stories. Certain other instincts and tendencies start developing by now. In order to be useful and successful, the text books should cater to these psychological needs with the following characteristics

(i) There is little scope for story telling and dialogues at this stage of education, as they should be different from the text-books, intended for the students of the Primary and the Junior High School Classes. There should be narration of facts in a realistic but interesting manner.

(ii) The subject matter of the text-books should be organised to satisfy the mental faculties of thinking, reasoning, imagination, etc.

(iii) The subject-matter should be properly selected to meet the requirements of the psychological needs of this stage of education.

(iv) Problems of social, political and moral value should form the subject matter of teaching at this stage of education, presented in an interesting and effective manner.

(v) As students of this age are fond of solving the problems, various problems concerning civic life should be presented before the students, through text-books, so they may take an active part in them and try to solve those.

(vi) For the students of Higher Secondary Classes text-books of Civics should have a good number of graphs and charts which are helpful in encouraging the students to take up serious study of civics.

(vii) There is scope for giving recent facts and figures in the text-books meant for this stage of education.

(viii) At this stage of education the language and the style of the text-books has a specific importance. The style should be lucid and well polished. The language should be easy conveying the thoughts properly and effectively. The subject-matter should be properly organised and categorised. The sequence of the sentence should not be very complex. An attempt should be made to present the subject matter in an attractive and effective style.

(ix) An attempt should be made to correlate the subject-matter of Civics with that of History, Political Science and such other social sciences that have a direct bearing on the subject-matter of Civics.

(x) As the subject-matter of Civics is more of a practical nature, an attempt should be made to employ Project Method, Problem Method, Activity Method, Excursion Method, etc., in its teaching. These methods should be made to reflect in text-books.

(xi) As every year we find some changes in the structure of the administration or the working of the civic life the subject-matter of Civics is of changing nature. Civics text-books should be kept up-to-date.

(xii) Civics text-books for this stage of education should be reasonable priced.

(xiii) There should be a set of psychologically planned and scientifically presented questions at the end of every chapter. These questions shall help the recapitulation of the subject matter.

In short, the text-book should meet all the requirements of this stage of education. According to Secondary Education Commission Report "We are greatly dissatisfied with the present standard of production of school books and consider it essential that it should be radically improved. Text-books of Civics are not very up-to date.

An attempt should be made to write text-books of civics to meet the requirements of each stage of education.

Recommendation of Patel Committee

The Committee has recommended that the number of pages in Civics text-books should be reduced to the minimum and that the language used should be easily understood by children of the particular age group.

Class VIII/IX-X

The Committee has recommended that in the area of Civics it is sufficient to provide a broad-based general education and that such correlation should be introduced as far as is natural and possible.

The Committee has suggested frames which give the main topics of civics and it will be for the States, local authorities, education/examination boards and schools to plan and fill in the details. Not suggesting uniform courses of study, Committee feels that "A single rigid scheme of studies for all schools may prove to be beyond the competence of some schools and may not provide a sufficient challenge to other schools. The content of courses, finally framed, must be capable of being taught or studied within the allotted time."

The committee has emphatically said that in civics, only the main ideas should be introduced; these should be few and important. Too many subjects need not be taught and whatever is taught should be taught thoroughly. Thus, the Committee believes that the main concepts in civics should be studied and that unnecessary details which overload the syllabus and lead to the memorising of scraps of information, should be avoided.

Supplementary Reading

In addition to the text-books and oral lessons delivered by the teacher, supplementary reading is of potential value for civics teaching. Whereas the text book aims at following the main currents of affairs hand in hand, the supplementary reading aims at throwing sidelights on the main topics. The text-book cannot satisfy all aspects of critical knowledge with regard to current references. Supplementary readers and other materials come up to fill up the lacunae. To quote Patel Committee report, "Recitations alone cannot possibly make up proper teaching of history, geography and civics. It is absolutely necessary from the earliest to the last grade that there should be a parallel reading of some kind." The teacher should have firmly fixed in his mind that it is impossible to teach civics without reference books as it is difficult to teach chemistry without glass apparatus and rubber tubes.

With only rare exceptions the text-books are not self-explanatory to the pupils and thus stand in need of elaboration by the teacher and through references books.

In bringing the past to the imagination of the pupils, older pupils books containing well-chosen extracts and anecdotes, can go a long way. Advanced works, reference books, source books, books on related subjects and allied fields- are very useful for older pupils because they will get a wide view of the subject in all its bearings.

Objectives of Supplementary Reading

1. To serve to widen the horizon of the learners and to add to their fund of knowledge.

2. To serve as a means for bringing out the relationship between the past and the present. The teacher should use the material from the dramas, letters, diaries, etc., to help in a conscious way to turn back the clock of time. "The essential condition," says Johnson, "is that they should leave feelings for and about the past."

3. To help in the enhancement of the information already acquired through the text-book. The pupil must be left on his own initiative to find what he ought to find and to report his independent summary in the class. He may be required to enter the main facts in his note-book.

4. To encourage the learner to form an acquaintance with historical literature. This should be so treated as to emphasise the record as well as the recorder.

5. To help the pupils form the conception of how social studies material is built up. This objective can be achieved through actual exercises in ciriticism and construction, requiring careful adjustments. The students should not be allowed to face hard and unspecified questions leading to unspecified answers. They should be encouraged to deal with the specified aspects of study and develop social and political consciousness.

6. To help in the self-study of the subject.

7. To help in making civics teaching more interesting and inspiring. Through the knowledge of supplementary studies a teacher can put life even in the dry text and break the monotony of his teaching work.

How to Make Supplementary Reading Useful ?

Freedom: A course in supplementary reading should be arranged scientifically and carried out without any element of compulsion. The teacher will do well to follow the suggestion of Johnson: "There should be no set questions to answer, no problems to solve, no looking forward to any formal report, but complete freedom to read because he likes it or to stop reading because he dislikes it." At the most, pupils may be encouraged to express their honest opinion when they feel inclined to do so.

Pleasure: If supplementary reading is to succeed, it must afford so much pleasure to the child that he is engrossed in it.

Inexpensive: The books forming the basis of extra reading should be inexpensive and easy to obtain.

Easy and lucid language: The language of supplementary readers and such other material must be easier than that of the text-book, to catch the interest of pupils.

Properly classified: The supplementary literature should be properly and scientifically classified and arranged in proper sequence.

Supplementing: The supplementary literature should aim to supplement the text-book and not convey the whole matter as given in the text.

According to the Psychological level: While suggesting books for extra reading, the teacher should bear in mind the mental capacity of his pupils. The pupils should be in a position to grasp the material presented in the book.

Truths not distortions: Supplementary literature should convey political and social truths and not a distortion of facts.

Clarity: Before making any suggestion for undertaking ancillary reading, the teacher must be definite about the following

(i) What types of optional or compulsory supplementary material is he to suggest?

(ii) Is the supplementary reading same for all the students or is it according to their various intellectual attainments?

(iii) Are the students to remain confined to one book or a small number of books or are they to be introduced to a large number?

(iv) How much reading is to be reasonably imparted?

(v) How should reading be arranged and assigned

(vi) How should reading be reported?

(vii) What devices should be pressed into service to maintain the interest once aroused?

Limits for the Teacher

(i) Avoid the wastage of time involved in making assignments.

(ii) Do not waste time in finding out the books. Every class should have a reserved shelf of its own to keep books. Alot separate period for the purpose.

(iii) Divide the class into groups and allow each group to make use of the library in that period.

(iv) Encourage pupils to keep their own record of supplementary reading they have gone through, putting down the following particulars in that record: (a) Author's name; (b) Name of the book; (c) Name of the publisher; (d) Newspapers or magazines read by them; (e) Extracts taken.

QUESTIONS

1. What is the importance of text books in the teaching of Civics? Bring out clearly the qualities and characteristics of the text books to be used in the teaching of Civics to Primary and Junior High School as well as Secondary classes.

2. What qualities do you expect in the Text-books of Civics at different stages of education?

12
Library, Museum and Laboratory

Objectives Laboratory

It has long been recognised that besides subjects like sciences and handicrafts Civics also requires a specially equipped laboratory for the objectives detailed below :

***To provide a home for Civics teacher*:** If the civics teacher is to be inspired with the requisite faith in himself, and imbued with essential imaginative strength, he should be provided with a home of his own. The most vital piece of apparatus in the civics laboratory is the civics teacher himself but if there is to be full scope for imaginative and practical methods of teaching, the provision of a "home of his own" is necessary to assist him to develop an enthusiasm for the subject and to provide him with best opportunities for awakening a corresponding interest in his pupils.

To create and maintain an effective atmosphere: Well-equipped with equipment and material for teaching civics a laboratory will create and maintain a much-needed atmosphere for civics. For example, the wall displays of varied nature can motivate the juniors, whereas the laboratory will provide a good activity centre for the seniors.

***To make Civics teaching more effective*:** Specialist accommodation give greater scope for variety in teaching methods and facilitates the use of teaching aids. The permanent display of important maps and globes, pictures and charts and constant reference to them by the civics teacher is sure to make the teaching of civics effective, lively and interesting.

To Provide a quick and ready civics functional environment: As mastery of essentials in civics extends beyond the theoretical knowledge, it is essential that there is provision for functional activities. The classroom facilities must be capable of rapid transformation into a laboratory setting. The physical equipment must provide a work room for the pupils, because activities and the practical solution of problems characterise, every unit or topic.

To save teaching time: Equipment like maps, models, charts, projectors, etc., is too cumbersome to carry around the school. A permanent base will save a lot of time. For instance, black-board can be prepared before hand, and the diagrams can be preserved for future use. The Civics laboratory is a highly desirable addition to any secondary school in which the teachers use a diverse methodology and go beyond the simple use of one text-book and a rigid curricular pattern.

Structure Laboratory

Size and amenities: The civics laboratory may be of any size. It should have good lighting and ventilation, adequate book cases and other storage facilities, tables and chairs to accommodate the students and teachers who are to work in it. With a proper arrangement for ventilation and light, the wall-space could be utilised for display of the chalk-board, bulletin board, models, maps and book-shelves. It should have the scope to serve as an audio-visual room as well.

Arrangement: Civics laboratory should be so arranged that it provides an inviting and stimulating atmosphere. It should be as much unlike the barewalled and fixed type of classroom as possible. The arrangement of furniture and display should be informal to give an impression that something interesting is happening in the room. It should look like a place where one is expected to do things, rather than recite formal lessons.

Furniture: The necessary items of furniture in a civics laboratory are working tables, chairs, shelves, stands, map-racks, almirahs and blackboards.

(i) ***Tables***: The tables should be small and flat and which can be easily rearranged for group work. The general arrangement of the room will be determined by the teacher and students, according to the immediate activity for learning such as discussion, forums, group work or viewing a film.

(ii) ***Seats***: Seating arrangements should be made for comfort, health and efficiency of the pupils. Individual desks or dual desks or tables and chairs should be moveable and easy to rearrange for a variety of purposes. Furniture should provide storage facilities for the pupil's books, pictures, etc.

(iii) ***Teacher's desk***: Teacher's desk should also be moveable, so that it may be used for general administration as well as instruction. It should be equipped with an atlas, a table dictionary, a memorandum pad and a desk-blotter.

(iv) ***Projection screen***: A permanent projection screen may be fixed above the black board which can be easily lowered for projection work any time. The windows should be provided with dark curtains which could be used when a film is to be screened.

(v) ***Channel railing***: A permanent channel railing with sliding hooks should be fixed along the chalk-board wall for hanging maps, pictures or graphs during teaching.

Equipment: A *Civics* laboratory should possess :

(i) ***Maps:*** historical, economic, political, social and pictorial maps of all the countries.

(ii) ***Charts:*** Different types of charts- Genealogy charts, Flow charts, Tabulation charts, Time charts, Relationship charts need to be provided. The charts may be purchased from the market or prepared by the teacher or pupils or both.

(iii) ***Time lines:*** Every civics laboratory should provide a time line which should run half-way along the wall. It should be painted or made of either the hard-board or card-board.

Important dates and persons should be marked appropriately all along with the line while teaching. The pictures of the important persons about whom the class is to study, can be nailed. This will help in making the pupils familiar with the distance between the lives of great persons.

(iv) ***Time graphs***: These may be provided to show the gradual and incidental rise and fall of the dynasties, the progress of rival powers, ideas and cultures, personages and movements.

(v) ***Models***: Civics laboratory should have models depicting sources of history, greatmen of different lands. Models can be prepared by the pupils under the guidance of the teacher. Ready-made models may also be purchased from the market.

(vi) ***Slide album***: Slides showing architecture, sculpture, paintings, dancing, music, etc., should also be there.

(vii) Flags of different nations of the world may be provided with explanatory notes.

(viii) ***Audio-visual aids***: Tape recorder, projector, filmstrip projector, Magic lantern, Epidiascope, etc., should also be provided.

(ix) ***Reference books***: Provision should be made for good historical novels, dramas, pictorial books, illustrating the life and customs of different peoples and important works of eminent writers. Some good books on civics besides biographies, auto-biographies and travel stories and encyclopaldias book on the peoples in different lands, etc., are also needed. These books should be always at hand when the subject is being taught.

(x) ***Bulletin board***: It is a necessary piece of equipment in civics laboratory because on it could be displayed relevant cuttings and pictures collected by pupils from magazines and newspapers. Maps, pictures, cartoons, newspaper reports on topics done or in progress in the classroom, can be displayed on the bulletin board with a caption or study questions for pupils.

However, complete with furniture and equipment no room will by itself make a perfect place for the proper study of civics. The laboratory must be extended by the wise teacher into the world outside, as far as he and his pupils can go, as a result of visits and all kinds of community contacts. He must understand that civics cannot be taught inside the laboratory, with the help of the text-book and by the teacher alone. Living and frequent contacts with the outside world will justify the purpose of the special laboratory for civics. The civics laboratory should become the hub of civics teaching and activities in a school. It should produce dynamic, sparkling interaction among physical things and students. It should be a place where ideas can come to life and be illustrated with activities and articles which help us to make the ideological experiences more lasting and pervasive in the lives of students as they continue on into the future.

Improvising Good Learning Environment

Some resourcefulness is required on the part of the teacher to make civics laboratory a miniature world to exhibit and to record the developments of explorations, research and discovery. A teacher should improvise and improvise well. A room, desk, charts and cupboards are the basic needs. He can tape the pictures to the wall, use the back of a map for a screen. Pictures can be collected from the old issues of magazines, weeklies, etc.

Civics laboratory should serve the purpose of a classroom, a library, a workshop, an amateur theatre, a students club, a stock room all rolled into one. It should grow steadily and constantly in equipment. It should become an interesting and exciting centre for activity for all the students and teacher's of civics in a school.

Civics Library

As an area of school curriculum civics demands a lot of reading on the part of both the teachers and the pupils. Therefore, is the utmost necessity to provide for book as well as non-book resources for the proper teaching and learning of civics.

Objectives of Library

1. To create interest in the subject.
2. To stimulate the students' mind into a fine restlessness.
3. To develop a critical attitude and a capacity for independent judgement.
4. To cultivate in the student a taste for extra reading
5. To acquaint the pupils with the various forms in which civics materials can be had.

Important Library Resources

Book resources: Books are essential for presenting different points of view, for providing adequate background for understanding the people, the processes and the places, so essential in civics instruction. Book, resources include :

***Textbooks*:** The library should have a variety of most up-to-date text-books in different sections of civics.

***Unit booklets*:** The booklets on a variety of topics, ranging from family life and neighbourhood to people of other lands and places, should be available in the library.

Library materials: Inspirational and imaginative literature, particularly tales of adventure, should appear prominently alongside books of information on children's hobbies- which may be anything from boats and balloons to kites or from doll houses to dress designs. Easy biographies, historical series, animal stories, etc., are favourites with children. Travel stories are really magic carpets to those who cannot leave their homes.

Reference Material

***Conventional*:** The library should be fairly well-equipped with reference materials-standard or conventional reference books and non-conventional reference books. Conventional reference books include dictionaries, encyclopaedias, year books, maps, charts, pamphlets, handbooks, manuals, syllabi of different classes, and books of knowledge. There should be some picture collections including well-known masterpieces and everything to which teachers and children are attracted.

Non-conventional: The non-conventional reference materials consist of all other library books that may be employed for reference service of any other kind. These include books on miscellaneous information and books -on special subjects-civics and political theory.

Non-book resources: The field of civics is concerned with happenings in the local community, the state, the nation and the world. Therefore it is essential that books are supplemented by periodicals, pamphlets, newspapers and other such materials which may help vitalise the teaching of civics with the latest in the field. The following non-book resources should be available in the social studies library.

***Periodicals*:** Some good periodicals and magazines throwing light on current events and various aspects of Indian life should be available in the library.

***Pamphlets*:** Pamphlets published by various Government agencies and bureaus for specialised service are also very important sources of information about different walks of life. They are generally low-priced. Every school library should subscribe to these.

***Newspaper*:** It is essential that the civics teacher and pupils keep well-informed of events of national and international importance. Some local newspapers and one or two other daily newspapers of all-India circulation need to be provided.

The library is the Intellectual Laboratory of the school. Textbooks are no longer 'Educational Bibles' to be used alone. They need to be supported, supplemented and reinforced by other sources of information. A library is the treasure vault of ideas, the store-house of knowledge, and the flowing stream of living thought. If civics is to be a living and vital discipline, the library must be accepted as an integral part of the entire social studies programme.

Utilization of library resources: Pupils should be taught the techniques of locating relevant references and resources material. Assignments should be given in the form of problems. This would compel the pupils to investigate and examine multiple sources. In the course of the search while pupils will assimilate some of the essential facts concerning the learning unit, they will be using these facts in a creative and productive way to arrive at their own independent conclusions, and thereby, invariably grow and enrich their knowledge, abilities, skills and interests.

Civics Museum

Museum is the temple of the Muse, intended to be a place for study. For ages, the museum has been regarded as the reference file of real objects by which to verify and amplify knowledge acquired and preserved in other forms.

Instruction through visits to museums is becoming increasingly popular in all progressive countries. Museums, especially those which preserve historical and cultural objects, impart wholesome education at all levels. They give new impetus to teaching methods. In most progressive countries, the museum is being recognised as an instrument of public education with vast potentialities. In Canada, a well-organised modern museum is considered essential to the educational system of the community. In Sweden, visits to museums are connected with the curriculum. Museum collections are a valuable aid to civics teachers in giving life and reality to school courses, at every stage of formal education. The organised class visits to the museum have been the accepted practice in most countries of Europe and America for several years. Guided tours, walk talks, and illustrated lectures supplement book-bound curriculum of schools.

Every school should have a museum with a separate section for each subject. There should be civics museum in each school to invest this area of school curriculum with a sense of reality. In civics, the preamble to our Constitution, Bill of Rights, Declaration of American Independence, etc., will enable the pupils to know something about the efforts of man for independence and a better way of life.

Sections of Museum

The material in a civics museum needs to be well-classified so that the pupils could get a fair idea of different events and developments. There can be three sections in the museum- local, national and international.

***The Local section*:** It may be built with local relics, local specimens, models, charts, etc. Images of gods and goddesses, carvings in bricks or stones, pottery pieces, ancient books, ancient coins, costumes, etc., can-build up this section. These can stimulate the interest of the pupils in the local history and civics and can invest the study with a sense of reality.

***The National section*:** It can be built up with the help of models as it may not be possible for each school to get original relics. Some commercial agencies in the country also supply educational models. The models can also be prepared by the pupils with the help of civics teacher. Models may be prepared on civilization of India during the New Stone Age, Indus Valley Civilization etc.

***The International section*:** Curios from different countries, stamps, coins, flags, dolls, etc., can be kept in this section.

The civics museum can be gradually built. Efforts should be made to find real objects which should be authentic but need not be valuable. There should also be models, photographs, diagrams, charts, paintings, etc. But the temptation to show too much must be cautiously resisted.

An elaborate account of each exhibit including the names of teacher and pupils responsible for the collection of the item, date, purpose, utilisation, expense and any other necessary information about it should be kept in a record book or in some other permanent form. The relics collected should be presented in chronological order with proper titles and annotations. The exhibits should be neatly displayed, the relics should be kept stocked in boxes and exhibited on appropriate occasions.

A good civics museum is not merely a collection of items, it should be a collection of useful items.

QUESTIONS

1. Why is it essential to have a Civics laboratory at a school? How will you furnish and equip it?
2. What should be the special features of a civics laboratory? Which of these would you leave out if you had only a moderate sum of money at your disposal?
3. A donor wishes to help you in equipping your Civics laboratory with books, furniture, etc., upto a limit of Rs. 2500. Draw up a list of your requirements. Ordinary furniture for the room is already provided.
4. The school library has a pivotal role in the modern instructional programme. How will you use library for effective teaching of Civics?
5. "Teaching of Civics at the Higher Secondary classes will remain ineffective and pointless without library resources." Discuss. Give a list of a dozen books in Civics which are a must for all the libraries.
6. Show the necessity of a Civics museum. How will you set about making it?
7. "A Civics museum is a great asset to a school." Elucidate, keeping in view the prescribed course of Civics for secondary classes in your state. Suggest ten items in order of importance that you will begin with for the development of Civics museum in your school.

13
Importance of Audio-Visual Aids

Need of Teaching Aids

Civics is an area of school curriculum that deals with both past and present time, immediate places and different corners of the world, people of the nearby locality and of different parts of the world. Mere chalking and talking will not help to make all these realistic and vivid before the pupils. A rich galaxy of audio-visual aids, must be harnessed to make the teaching of civics lively and interesting. A variety of aids like pictures, maps, films, filmstrips, models, cartoons, charts, graphs, etc. will give a welcome relief from normal routine.

The Advantages

Supplementing the spoken word. Civics teaching deals with words which go beyond the experience of pupils. The teaching uses a vocabulary mentioning people of different times and climes. Mere verbal descriptions will not help to bring the facts home to the pupils. To supplement and explain the spoken word, the teacher must take the help of audio-visual aids.

Making Civics real, vivid, vital, interesting and life-like. As an area of curriculum civics is not popular with pupils due to its dead uniformity and frozen and fixed account of facts. There is an urgent necessity to uplift the teaching of civics. The use of audio-visual aids can add zest, interest and vitality to any teaching-learning situation and invigorate the teaching of civics.

Developing concepts, improving attitudes and extending appreciations and interests. The presentation of civics through various devices helps in portraying the matter in the true and realistic form. When there is something to see and hear, it helps in the development of proper concepts, improvement of attitudes and extension of appreciations and interests.

Making learning permanent. As potent starters and motivators teaching aids compel the pupils to attend and learn faster,, remember longer and gain more accurate information.

Supplementing the material of the text-books. Civics text books lack the specificity, the warmth, and the unutterable poignancy of concrete experiences. Direct purposeful experiences supply the context for sound and skilful generalising and help in better understanding of the text-books. Thus, civics rises above the civics text-book.

Audio-visual aids are supplementary devices by which the teacher of civics can help to clarify, establish and correlate accuracy, concepts, interpretations and appreciations through the utilisation of more than one sensory channel to make civics alive -and interesting.

Types of Teaching Aids

Teaching aids are devices presenting units of knowledge through auditory or visual stimuli or both to help learning. Concretising the knowledge to be presented they help in making a learning experience appear real, living and vital. They supplement the work of the teacher and help in the study of text-books.

Basing his classification of teaching aids upon the kinds of experiences presented through them Edgar Dale presents a "Cone of Experience." The range of audio-visual aids, is between direct experience and pure abstraction. These divisions are not rigid, they overlap and blend into each other. The cone is a `visual metaphor' of learning experiences depicting the various items in the order of increasing abstractions as one proceeds from direct purposeful experience which is the bedrock of all education. The second stage involves the use of contrivances like models. Dramatics invoke a reconstructed experience where contrivances fail. Participation is better than mere watching. Observation comes upper-most and includes items like demonstrations, field trips, exhibits, motion pictures, radio, recordings and pictures. In these, the pupils simply watch and listen. Aids like film projectors, radio and epidiascope fall in this category.

Verbal symbols signify that a certain word stands for an object, action or thing. The symbol can be anything from a word and idea to a formula and philosophic aphorism.

Galaxy of Teaching Aids

Printed Aids

1. Periodicals
2. Books
3. Newspapers

Visual Aids

4. Slides
5. Film strips
6. Models
7. Graphs and Charts
8. Pictorial materials
9. Globes and Maps

Audio-Aids

10. Tape Recordings
11. Phonograph discs
12. Radio

Audio-Visual Aids

13. Motion Pictures

14. Television
15. Dramatisation.

The Characteristics

I.K. Davies has suggested the following five characteristics of audio-visual aids:

(i) Developing perception.

(ii) Developing understanding, enabling the pupils to acquire correct knowledge.

(iii) Helping in transfer or training.

(iv) Helping in acquiring knowledge and providing reinforcement.

(v) Developing retention and facilitating assimilation of the knowledge.

Importance and Functions

Motivation: Audio-visual aids present civics knowledge in the concrete form by attracting the attention of the pupils. It provides motivation and curiosity to the pupils in the learning activity. The pupils listen with attention and learn easily the lesson taught by audio-visual aids.

Activity: Doing various activities by using audio-visual aids, the pupils talk, ask questions and discuss. As this stimulates their various sense organs, their interest in the lesson sustains and they learn the most difficult things in a natural way without any difficulty.

Clarification: The use of audio-visual aids clarifies the most difficult contents because whatever the pupils hear, they also see it with their own eyes. This eliminates all the confusions and they acquire the knowledge with precision.

Meaningful Experience: A lesson is taught to the pupil in a concrete form with the help of audio-visual aids. He tries to understand correctly by seeing and touching the object. This makes the lesson easy, interesting and entertaining. Thus, the use of audio-visual aids makes the experiences of the pupils meaningful and encourages original thinking. The symbolic representation of direct experience is possible by means of audio-visual aids.

Discouragement to Cramming: As the pupils take interest in the development of the lesson by using audio-visual aids and they acquire the knowledge by doing themselves, there is no need of cramming anything. This makes the learnt knowledge definite and stabilized.

Increase in Vocabulary: The use of audio-visual aids increases vocabulary of the pupils because new terms are used and acquired while using radio, telephone, television and cinema.

Efficiency in Teaching: The use of audio-visual aids provides efficiency in teaching and makes it more effective. Minute things and difficult ideas are followed easily by using audio-visual aids. Dry and uninteresting subjects and topics are made easy, interesting and precise by using audio-visual aids.

Various Types

Audio Aids

Audio-aids are those sources of teaching in which only hearing organs are used and knowledge gained mainly through the ears, as much as radio, gramophone and tape-recorder. .

Radio: The story of the radio's birth started from 1885. In the modern life radio has become our need. It provides knowledge of latest events and informations to all the pupils living at far off places. It arouses curiosity of learning new things in the pupils. It provides talks and speeches of eminent educationists on national and international problems developing international feeling among pupils. They understand and solve the problems of daily life. Radio creates interest in the pupils regarding every nation and the activities of the people. It broadens their general knowledge. Most of the schools have their own individual radio-sets.

Gramophone: Pupils are given training for speech by gramophone. The teacher should use it during teaching as the need arises. After using these devices the teacher must provide clarifications of the subject to the pupils.

Tape-recorder: In tape-recorder anybody can hear his or others' recorded voice. Thus tape-recorder is used to hear the ideas of great men and speeches of leaders. The pupils and the teachers may also hear their recorded voice.

Visual Aids

Visual aids are those sources in which only visual organs are used or applied and knowledge is mainly achieved through visual organs. These are as follows: .

Real objects: Actual objects means original objects which motivate the sense organs of the pupils and develop their power of observation by providing the opportunities of supervision and testing. When the pupils see real objects, touch them and taste them, their .visual, taste, touch and hearing powers develop. These powers or talents help in developing their power of imagination. Thus by using the real objects pupils acquire various types of experiences provided by others. The teacher should collect real objects in the civics museum so that these can be exhibited to the pupils as the need arises.

Models: Models are the miniature forms of real or original objects used when the real objects are either beyond availability or so huge that these are impossible to be exhibited in the class. Hence, models are presented to the pupils for the knowledge of such objects. Models should be the exact copy of the real objects irrespective of their size. Sometimes models are better than the real objects because these can be seen properly. Close to the real objects in structure, models help in developing the power of imagination and in providing the knowledge to the pupils regarding historical and scientific facts.

Pictures: Pictures are used when neither the real objects nor models are available. The real touch of the real object does not occur in the picture. Still pictures are useful in teaching. These are cheaper than models and real objects and are easily available in the market. When the teacher imparts knowledge with the help of pictures, the pupil's attention remains focussed on the lesson. Hence, the teacher must use pictures in lower classes. Though the pictures should be used in teaching all the subjects, but these should be used especially in the teaching of civics. If the ready-made pictures are not available, the teacher should prepare them himself in order to clarify the things related to the lesson. While selecting the pictures; the teacher should follow the following points:

(i) The pictures should be precise, coloured and attractive so that the pupils become familiar with the size and shape of the real objects.

(ii) Only relevant things should be shown in picture otherwise the main points will be side-tracked and the pupils will get confused.

(iii) The size of the picture should be so large that every pupil sitting in the class may see it clearly without any difficulty.

Maps: The use of maps is essential to study the main historical events, facts and places. The teacher should prepare them himself and mark only those things which are required. He must write the name, heading, direction and symbol, etc., on the maps. Colours should be used with imagination, experience and artistic sense.

Sketches and Diagrams: If the teacher fails to acquire real objects, models, pictures and maps, he should draw sketches and diagrams on the black-board with the coloured chalks to make the sense distinct. The teacher must possess the ability of drawing sketches and diagrams quickly. As there are no expenses in drawing the sketches and diagrams, every teacher should practise it.

Graphs: By using graph, knowledge of civics can be imparted conveniently. Graph may show climate, cultivation and population etc. They can be used in imparting the knowledge of the freedom-struggle and development in the religious and political fields. While teaching civics the teacher may also get these graphs drawn.

Charts: The charts can be used successfully in civics. Keeping in mind the needs of the lesson, the teacher should himself prepare large-sized charts and use them properly. The content presented in the charts should be beautiful, bold and large-sized attracting every student towards it so that the teacher may clarify his point easily.

Black Board: Black board means a black wooden piece usually 48"x36", also placed on a table and used in the- class at the time of teaching. It can also be shifted out of the class-room as the need arises. Sometime a board of 72"x48" size is made of cement on the wall: A wooden board of the same size may be fixed on the wall. Black Board is a must for civics class.

The black-board is the cheapest instrument of civics teaching. If the teacher writes important points on the black-board while teaching orally, then alongwith the sense of hearing, the sense of sight of the pupil also becomes active. Therefore, the black-board is considered an important device in the teaching of civics. It is used to develop teaching points in civics and to write the summary, and draw the diagrams. All the pupils understand the terms, facts, events, pictures and summaries etc. written on the black-board very easily. The teacher is comfortable in assigning the home work and teaching the whole class at a time with the help of black-board. Thus, both the pupils and the teacher are benefitted. As the pupil considers the written matter on the black-board as a model, they follow it and get impressed. The teacher and the pupil-teacher must use black-board while teaching civics.

Rules about the use of Black Board

Neat, beautiful and clear writing: The teacher should have a good handwriting. He should know how to write difficult words, meanings, facts; events and summaries in a neat, beautiful and legible manner.

Bright letters: The teacher should write bright letters so that every pupil may read the written letters easily. For this, he should write on black-board with white instead of coloured chalks. The letters written with coloured chalks are not so bright and many pupils are unable to read them. Letters written with white chalks are bright enough.

Straight writing: The teacher should write on black-board in a straight line. The pupils may read it without strain on their eyes. They can read the writing successfully. Writing in oblique lines looks very bad. Therefore the pupil-teachers should write in straight lines.

Size of letters: The teacher should write neither very large-sized nor too small letters. Size of his writing should be such that even the back-bencher pupils may read it easily. Some teachers write very large-sized or too small sized letters on the black-board. As the pupils cannot read very small letters easily, they get bored from the lesson. The pupils may laugh at the large-sized letters written on the black-board, which may spoil the class-room discipline.

System of writing: The system of writing on the black-board should be appropriate, enabling the pupils to understand the written things easily and copy them on their note-books for revision at home. When the system of writing on black-board is not appropriate but haphazard the pupils don't take interest in it. They acquire incorrect knowledge.

Use of One language only: Some teachers use both Hindi and English letters which make pupils confused. The teacher should use only one language on black-board.

Speed of writing: The teacher should write speedily on the black-board. If he writes very slowly it delays the lesson. Speed in writing does not mean committing error or mistake in writing as it makes the teacher an object of joke for the pupils or they will acquire incorrect knowledge. Therefore the teachers should write rapidly and carefully.

Distance between Teacher and black board: The teacher should stand at such a distance from the black-board so that he may read his own writing conveniently and make corrections immediately.

Use of duster: To rub off the written matter on the blackboard the teacher should use a duster.

Talking while writing: While writing on the black-board the teacher should keep on talking about the written words and sentences. All the pupils note down all the facts after understanding properly. Class room discipline is maintained because the attention of all the pupils is concentrated in writing alongwith the teachers. Pupils don't take much time to write. Hence, the chalk and talk of the teacher should go side by side while using black-board.

Use of pointer: The pupil-teachers and teachers should use a pointer to explain the writing on the black-board to their pupils pointing out with their own fingers.

An eye on the class: While writing on black-board he should see whether all the pupils are doing their task quietly or not. If he finds some pupils talking, he should supervise their task. This will stop talking and the pupil would be cautious for future.

Opportunities for students to use black-board: Some teachers consider the black-board for them only and not for pupils. It is a mistake. They should provide opportunities to the pupils to use the black-board for writing some important points on it. This helps the pupils to maintain their concentration, to eliminate their hesitation and to have self-confidence, self-dependence and efficiency.

Bulletin board: On Bulletin board are displayed the informations regarding a country's political, economic and social problems along with pictures, graphs, diagrams, articles and necessary information arousing pupil's curiosity and increasing their knowledge. The following points should be kept in mind to benefit from bulletin board:

(i) The material displayed on bulletin board should be in accordance with the interest, mental level, age and ability of the pupils.

(ii) The information displayed on the bulletin board should be managed in a definite order or sequence.

(iii) The material displayed on the bulletin board should be large enough for the pupils to see it from a distance.

(iv) Bulletin board should be fixed at an appropriate place in the school so that the pupils of average height may benefit conveniently from the displayed material.

(v) Bulletin boards should be beautiful so that the pupils are attracted automatically.

(vi) The pupils also must have the opportunity of displaying their collected material on the Bulletin boards.

Flannel board: Flannel boards are prepared by mounting a flannel cloth tightly on a 36"x48" piece of plywood or hard board. On it are displayed pictures, maps, sketches and graphs etc. related to different subjects. Sand papers åre pasted on the back of the pictures and maps etc in order to display on the flannel board. This makes them sticking to the flannel board. These can be removed very easily after using them. Flannel boards can be used very conveniently for teaching civics.

Museum: An important device of teaching, it includes collected objects in which a lesson becomes alive and interesting and the pupils understand easily. The teacher must make the best use of the museum in the teaching of civics. He should encourage the pupils to collect objects for the school museum.

Magic lantern: The Magic Lantern is a picture exhibiting device, which has proved much useful and successful in making the teaching alive and effective. After providing knowledge regarding various subjects to the pupils in the morning, they are used to show slides relating to those subjects in the evening.' This makes it easy to acquire knowledge while forgetting would be minimized. The magic lantern is an important source to make the abstract facts and deep ideas understandable. The teacher should observe the following precautions while using magic lantern:

(i) Before showing slides, he should present some background regarding the subject.

(ii) While showing slides, he should provide some interpretations or inferences.

Epidiascope: Epidiascope is a more effective device than magic lantern to make the lesson precise and interesting. While the magic lantern needs the preparation of slides before showing pictures, in the case of epidiascope he can project small maps, pictures, posters and pages of books on a screen in the dark room without preparing any slide. As Epidiascope magnifies micro-picture very easily, it has an, important place in the modern education system in teaching civics. In rich countries like America and England, the epidiascopes are used in order to make the lesson ,interesting and precise. But in India due to financial restrictions the pupils are devoid of its benefits. The teacher should observe the following precautions while using epidiascope:

(i) Screen should be arranged.

(ii) The room should be darkened where it is to be used.

(iii) The size of the pictures to be projected should be according to the epidiascope.

(iv) The class-room environment should be peaceful.

(v) Notes should be given so that the pupils gain clear knowledge about the subject.

Slides, film strips and projector: Micro informations can be magnified on the screen with the help of slides. While showing slides, the teacher clarifies minute details by his statements. This simplifies the lesson and makes it interesting. Slides are made on glass and are very delicate and heavy. Now slides are being produced on film and film strips. 15-20 slides relating to some lesson are transferred on photographic film on 35 mm in order to prepare film strip. This film is projected with the help of a projector in the class-room on a screen. This makes the lesson alive. Hence, projector is more important than epidiascope because with epidiascope only individual objects can be shown separately while the slides of the pictures or film strips are shown in a sequence. Pictures relating to different subjects can be shown at different intervals of time with the help of a projector as the need arises.

Soundless motion pictures: Soundless picture is a primitive form of a motion picture which shows complete activities but lacks sound. Hence, it is an important aid.

Teaching machines: Originally, B.F Skinner developed the teaching machine for the presentation of instructions. Prof. S.L. Pressey of Ohio State University developed teaching machine for the first time. They developed many teaching and testing machines. Pressey felt that pupils can learn on his machine by testing. Pressey and his students published many articles including details of various designs of machines and their evaluation.

Originally, Pressey followed multiple choice items in his machine. The pupil is provided with four alternate answers for a single question. Out of these four, only one answer happens to be correct. The pupil selects one opinion out of these four opinions as his response. If the answer of the pupil is correct, then the machine provides him next question. If the answer is not correct, the pupil goes on trying till he seeks right answer.

Observing that these machines saved labour and evaluation time along with measurable learning-growth, Pressey developed many models of recording devices.

Types of Teaching Machines

Many types of programmed instructional material is presented by teaching machines. Teaching Machines are of two types :

(i) ***Auto instructional device***: In these types projected and non-projected machines are included, such as radio, television, motion picture etc.

(ii) ***Linear teaching machine:*** Linear instructional material is studied in this type of teaching machine.

The Characteristics

(1) Various types of instructions can be presented.

(2) The content produced is handed over to the teaching machine after its construction and evaluation.

(3) The pupils are informed whether their responses are correct or incorrect. This restrains them from copying.

(4) Record of pupils responses gives estimates about how much the pupil has studied and how many correct and in correct responses he has produced.

(5) The teaching problems are solved.

(6) Opportunities for external responses provided. The pupil writes his responses and verifies them.

The Advantages

(1) The pupils get the opportunities of learning according to individual differences.

(2) There is a provision of reinforcement.

(3) The pupils do not indulge in copying.

(4) The achievements of the pupils are evaluated.

(5) The teaching task of the teachers is simplified.

(6) The pupil's behaviour is controlled.

(7) The pupil's responses cannot be altered.

(8) A correct record of the pupils' responses is maintained.

(9) The objective data relating to the learning process is collected for research work.

Limitations

(i) These are much costlier.

(ii) The repairing is very much costly.

(iii) The fingers and hands of the pupils get injuries by using them.

(iv) Pupils' training is affected by their break-down.

Material Aids in Teaching

Peculiarities of age: Children between 6 to 11 years of age receive education at this stage of education. Their social, moral, mental and physical education does not take place simultaneously and at the same speed but differs from child to child. As the children grow, their physical and mental organs develop. Therefore, it is not possible to employ one set of teaching aids to all the students simultaneously. It should differ from stage to stage.

Primary education is the stage of early childhood. Children are fond of listening to stories., Curiosity is their predominant instinct. The teacher should try to impart education by playing upon curiosity of the children. Civics education should be of a concrete nature. Attempt should be made to make the teaching interesting and attractive. Various types of teaching aids should be employed, bearing in mind the consideration of the mental and the physical age group of the children.

Textbooks: This is not the stage when children may be taught with the text-books. The text-books may be used only for helping the students to revise and strengthen the experiences given to them in the class room. The text-books used should be well illustrated, attractive and nicely printed.

Models: Generally Panchayats, Zila Parishads etc. are taught at this stage of education. Models of these should be presented before the students. These models should be attractive and artistic. Students should be encouraged to prepare such models. This shall encourage their learning by, doing.

Pictures and charts: Pictures should be used at this stage of education as they satisfy the curiosity of the students. While using these pictures, it should be remembered that they should be accurate, artistic and attractive. Neatly drawn charts may also be used.

Black-board: Black board plays an important role at this stage of teaching Civics. Various things should be put down on the black-board, and then illustrated orally. Charts may be drawn on these boards. An attempt should also be made to write legibly. Maps and charts should also be neatly drawn.

Home task: Home task is not advisable at this stage of education.

Junior High School

Peculiarities of Age: At this stage of civics teaching children are between the age group of 11-14. This may be called the boyhood. Next stage is adolescence. At this stage children have thinking, reasoning and such other mental faculties developed. An attempt should be made to make civics teaching more realistic at this stage. This should be well reflected in the use of teaching aids.

Textbooks: Text-books are the traditional aids to be used at this stage of education.

Charts and Pictures: At this stage of education pictures do not have great value as an aid but charts do have a value. An attempt should be made to encourage the students to draw charts.

Models: As Models are useful at this stage of education, an attempt should be made to encourage the students to construct models.

Audio-visual Aids: Audio-visual Aids like radio, tape recorder, film etc. may also be employed at this stage of education.

Black-board: Black-board should be properly used at this stage. Graphs and maps etc. may be drawn on the board. The students may be asked to fill in things on the maps and graphs.

Bulletin board: It may be used for pasting pictures and cartoons, etc., useful for the teaching of Civics.

Secondary Stage of Civics Teaching

Peculiarities of age: At this stage of education the teachers have to teach the students who have a good deal of physical, moral and mental development. At this stage they have reached adolescence. They do not very much need the teaching aids. Things may be given to them in a realistic manner. However, teaching aids may not be fully discarded at this stage of civics teaching. These should be employed, with a bit of realistic touch.

Textbooks: Text-books must be utilised at this stage of teaching civics. The students should be asked to use the text-books in doing home task.

Black-board: Black-board should be utilised for putting down the substance of the topic taught in the class and for presenting facts before the students.

Audio-visual Aids: Various audio-visual aids may be utilised for imparting civics education in a successful manner at this stage of education.

QUESTIONS

1. What are teaching aids? How are they useful in civics teaching?
2. Enumerate and explain the important teaching aids that may profitably be employed by the teacher of civics in different classes of schools.
3. Keeping in view the need of practical work and experience, both in school and outside, explain some of the teaching aids that can be employed in the teaching of civics at the senior stage in our schools.
4. The primary purpose of models and pictures in the teaching of civics is to give definiteness to visual imagery. Comment. Bring out the utility of models and pictures for primary classes in civics teaching.

5. Discuss the importance of excursion as an aid for teaching civics. Plan an excursion programme for the students of the IX class and then show how the knowledge so gained is more useful than what students should have learnt in the classroom.
6. What is the importance of the following aids in the teaching of civics? What precautions should we take while using them?
7. What use would you make of maps, timelines and charts in teaching civics to high school students? Select a suitable topic from the X class syllabus to illustrate your procedure.
8. Highlight the use of Material Aids in Civics Teaching at various stages.

14

Planning the Lessons

In the words of Lester B. Sands, "A lesson-plan is actually a plan of action. It, therefore, includes the working philosophy of the teacher, her knowledge of philosophy, her information about and understanding of her pupils, her comprehension of the objectives of education, her knowledge of the material to be taught, and her ability to utilise effective methods." A lesson-plan is the statement of the achievements to be realised and the specific means by which these are to be attained as a result of the activities engaged in, during the period. A lesson plan points out what has already been done, in what direction the pupils should next be guided and helped and what work is to be taken up immediately. "It is the teacher's mental and emotional visualization of the classroom experience as she plans it to occur." In many ways, it is the core, the heart of effective teaching.

A lesson-plan should tell the story, the way the teacher intends to employ children for a given period- what he/she and they are going to do. This written 'programme' shows both sincerity and a flexible and informal plan.

In lesson plan, the teacher is playing the chief role in a performance. Therefore the plan should look more like a programme with bold headings and lesser headings indicating the different things that are to go on at different times, who are to do those things, what aids are to be used, and a certain amount of what is to be said.

The Advantages

Careful lesson-planning, the foundation of all good teaching, has the following advantages :

Selection: It involves consideration of goals and objectives, the selection of subject-matter and the selection of procedure. It is the planning of activities and the planning of evaluation devices.

Planning: Lesson Planning keeps the teacher on the track, ensures steady progress and a definite outcome of teaching and learning procedures.

Effective teaching: Through lesson planning the teacher looks ahead and plans a series of such activities as will progressively modify students' attitudes, habits, information and abilities in desirable directions.

Prevents waste: Lesson planning helps the teacher to be systematic and orderly. It encourages proper organisation of subject matter and activities and prevents haphazard teaching. It eliminates disorder and other ills of thoughtless teaching.

Checks for forgetting: A lesson plan ensures that the teacher does not forget a vital point. It reminds him of the telling phrases, the apt quotations, effective similes or illustrations at the right moment in the lesson.

Confidence: Through lesson plan the teacher can enter the class without anxiety, ready to embark with confidence upon a job he understands and prepared to carry it to workman-like conclusion.

Provides check lesson plan: It serves as a check on unplanned curriculum.

Provides framework: A lesson plan provides a framework to help the work, directing along the lines of the syllabus at a suitable rate. The hierarchy of lessons is made well-knit and interconnected. Continuity is assured while needless repetition is avoided.

Opportunity for professional work: Though lesson planning entails hard work, it is the most rewarding sort of professional work that a teacher can do. Through lesson planning, the teacher gets on opportunity to use his skill, intelligence, ability and opportunity to become a successful teacher.

The Principles

Care and flexibility: The teacher should prepare a careful but flexible plan. He should be free to change the plan as required by the developing lesson and the needs of the children. The plan should be used as a guide rather than as a rule of thumb to be obeyed blindly. The teacher should have the courage to depart from the plan as and when the needs of his students demand.

Mastery and training: The teacher must have mastery of and adequate training in the topic from which the subject-matter has been selected for a certain lesson.

Skill in methods and techniques/planning: The teacher must be fully conversant with new methods and techniques of teaching civics.

Based on pupil's Psychology: In planning a lesson, the teacher must know his pupils thoroughly and organise the materials in a psychological rather than merely a logical fashion. In order to know how to provide for them, he must understand his pupil's traits and interests.

Participation of students: The teacher must ensure active participation of students.

Absence of monotony: Work during a lesson should be varied, particularly with young pupils. On different occasions or at different stages of the lesson in the same period, this variety of work may be marked by pupil's writing, watching, doing or listening to some person.

Various Steps in Lesson-Planning

For teaching civics effectively, the teacher has to proceed in a systematic manner. Although there can be no rigidity about them, following steps have to be followed in preparing a lesson plan in civics.

Formulation of educational objectives (Aims): While planning a lesson the teacher should ask himself the following questions :

(i) Is this lesson primarily one of attitudes, skills, concepts, or knowledge? Or is it a combination of two or more of these?

(ii) If he has to get just one idea or attitude or skill of concept across today, what should it be? What does he want them to know when students leave the classroom. As is so well said by Leonard Kenworthy, "What is the bull's eye" of the teaching target for today?"

(iii) What are one or two other major aims? Are these aims suitable for this class or far beyond their level of comprehension, or possibly behind them?

(iv) Are these aims specific?

The teacher should remember that the specific aims are determined in their relationship to general aims. He should think out as to what he intends to do in that particular lesson, *e.g.*, to enable the pupils to be familiar with the rights and duties of the citizen in India.

Selection and Organisation of Content: For selection and organisation of content the teacher should put the following questions to himself

(i) What type of content should be selected to achieve the intended objectives.?

(ii) How can the present knowledge of the pupils be used to make the lesson meaningful and interesting to them? How can the teacher arrange the relevant facts in order to relate them to the lives of the students?

(iii) How much time may be spent in discussion, revision, practical work or in disciplinary interruptions. This will enable the teacher to arrange rate of exposition.

(iv) How can he start this lesson? How can he use this motivation throughout the lesson?

(v) How can he reach the slow students? How can he reach the fast students?

(vi) What materials or aids can he best use? Are these materials suitable for all the students?

(vii) How can he summarise the lesson?

(viii) What home-work should be given to the students?

Motivation or Preparation: In this step, the word motivation has been used in two different ways

As a broad approach to teaching: This motivation includes all that the teacher knows about learning. It is something that goes on during the period. It comes from the teacher's use of his voice, from questioning, relating the past to the present, and many other sources.

***As a way of getting a lesson under way*:** This motivation means the ways of getting a lesson started, getting a lesson "off the ground" so to speak.

Ways to Motivate the Pupils for the New Lesson

***Using objects*:** Costumes, coins, sculpture pieces, pictures, etc., may be used to start a topic.

***Opening with a startling statement of question*:** At the beginning of the lesson, the teacher makes the statement-Democracy is the government of the people, by the people and for the people. The rest of the period can be spent in discussing how this statement is true.

***Using socio-drama*:** The teacher announces that he wants volunteers for positions in the session of National Parliament. Some pupils may volunteer to play one role, some others may play other roles. In this way, pupils may be motivated for discussion on working of Lok Sabha. Individuals may be selected or asked to volunteer to represent the great freedom fighters. They may be asked to make brief statement on how they contributed in the struggle of Indian Independence. An assignment to learn about the role-playing should be given to the pupils in advance for this type of lesson. These roles should be maintained throughout the lesson.

Posing a problem: As soon as the class starts, the teacher says that war has started in Kargil sector of Kashmir. He should then ask the students how the Indian citizen should contribute to win it. The rest of the period can then be spent in discussing the details of citizen's duties during war.

Using a filmstrip or film: Certain very good filmstrips and films are available which can be used to motivate students.

Using the chalk-board: At the start of the period or before the students have entered the room, the teacher draws a pyramid on board. Then he suggests that this represents the Indian people at the time of 1947 when British were to quit India. During the rest of the period, the class fills in this chart with the Prime Minister, and other leaders. A discussion can then describe how Indians took over the reins of government in their own hands from the Britishers.

It may be remembered here that all the lessons need not have a startling opening. Motivation also comes from intrinsic interest aroused in scores of ways over a long period of time. The techniques suggested above, give an illustration of how teachers can arouse and maintain interest in the lesson throughout a period.

Student's activity and teacher's role: In a period there should be a fair distribution of time between student's and teachers' activity. The teacher may keep his pupils active by frequent questions fairly distributed over the whole of the class. The pupils may also be encouraged to ask questions. Thus, learning should be a two-way process. The pupils should be active participants in the learning process. It is helpful to keep a record of pupil participation.

(i) To see how many questions are coming from them.

(ii) To see who is taking maximum part in class discussion and who is taking minimum part.

(iii) To see if there are parts of the lesson that the teacher is neglecting.

Recapitulation: Without a recapitulation assignment, lesson is an incomplete one. The principal purpose of recapitulation is to make the presentation more effective. It helps the pupils to arrive at some conclusion with reference to the wider significance of the problem. An attempt is made to ask children to "tell back" or reproduce what they have learnt. The pupils learn how to express themselves and how to reproduce the material learnt.

Assignment: Out of the work done assignment is essential for the consolidation of knowledge. The pupils should do some exercise in the form of answers to some objective or essay type questions, draw the maps and indicate the important places, collect the statements, sayings or couplets of great leaders and saints, prepare scrapbooks, write out reports, etc.

Chalk-board work: While the lesson is expected to be learnt in class, it is necessary for the pupils to have some record of it with them for future reference. A brief outline of the lesson shall be more precise and concrete to them. Therefore, the teacher should make a chalk-board summary of most lessons.

This should be brief, precise, neat and systematic and cover the whole lesson. As it is difficult for the teacher to develop it off hand in the class, it is always best to think out the chalk-board summary before hand and put it down in the lesson note for reference.

Except in very elementary cases, Chalk-board summary should be in the form of an outline. It is only a frame of reference for the pupils for guidance in their studies. While it should cover the whole lesson it should be made only in points and sub-points. Proper heads for the points and sub-points become self-evident even without the help of complete sentences. As far as possible Chalk-board summary should be developed with the help of pupil. Chalk-board work may also include sketches, outline diagrams, maps, graphs, pictures, time lines and directions.

Teacher's self evaluation or evaluation of lesson plan: After a lesson is completed, it should be evaluated by asking following questions and filling in the columns to the right with comments.

Chalk-board work may also include sketches, outline diagrams, maps, graphs, pictures, time lines and directions.

As far as possible Chalk-board summary should be developed with the help of pupils

Question	*Yes*	*No*	*Comments*
1. Was the motivation effective?			
2. Could I maintain this motivation throughout the lesson?			
3. Were the aims clear to the pupils?			
4. Did I have the right number of aims?			
5. Were my questions effective and well distributed?			
6. Were there questions from the class during the period?			
7. Was my command and mastery over the subject sound to enable me to change the plan where necessary?			
8. Did I use some effective audio-visual aids?			
9. Was I able to involve the slower and quieter students?			
10. Was I able to satisfy and challenge the superior students?			
11. If I did not know something, did I call on the class for help or promise to look it up?			

12. Did I try to repeat or review or use facts from time to time to drive the facts home to the pupils?
13. Was there enough pupil participation?
14. Did I include a home-work assignment?

Views of Herbart on Lesson Plan- Herbart introduced the system of Lesson Plan. He was an idealist who believed in imparting education to the students for building up their character. In order to achieve this objective, he gave an important place to the teacher in the educational set-up. He provided a general method to be utilised by the teachers for imparting knowledge to the students in the class-room. With the help of this method Herbart achieved the objective of building of the character of the students.

Herbart laid down the following four steps in his method of teaching. According to him the Lesson Plan or the method of teaching should have the following traits :

(1) Clearness or clarity;

(2) Association;

(3) System; and

(4) Method.

Improvement by Zillar- Zillar, a disciple of Herbart, made an attempt to improve Herbart's method of the teaching. He divided the step of clearness into two further sub-divisions; namely, (a) Introduction and (b) Presentation.

Thus, Herbart's whole plan is known as five steps of Herbart. It was found very useful in the teaching of Science and Mathematics, with certain modifications, it can also be utilised for the teaching of other subjects as well. In the following pages Herbart's method has been used in drawing of the lesson plans of Civics.

GENERAL OUTLINE OF A LESSON PLAN IN CIVICS

Lesson Plan No ....

Name of the Institution ....

Day and Date- Class
Subject- Period
Topic- Average age
Time -
Name of the pupil-teacher ....

The General Aims should be put down after writing all these things. These General Aims are almost the same in all the lessons. The aims of the teaching Civics is to achieve these aims or objectives. They are given below :

General Aims

(1) To inculcate the spirit of ideal citizenship.

(2) To teach the students the rights and duties of the citizens and the State.

(3) To teach students the lesson of self-control.

(4) To inculcate in the students the feeling of world brotherhood or world fraternity.

(5) To enable the students to grow into useful citizens of the society.

(6) To create and develop the interest for the study of the Civics in the students.

(7) To bring about the development of the qualities of sympathy, sacrifice, co-operation and character in the students.

(8) To develop the power of thinking, reasoning, imagination and decision in the students.

(9) To develop scientific outlook in the students.

Specific Aims

These aims have a direct bearing on the topic or the subject-matter to be taught in the class-room. They should be presented in a simple, and concise form.

Teaching Aids

(1) These are the devices by which the lessons are made interesting and effective.

(2) It is not necessary to use these aids in each and every lesson. They should be used as and when required.

(3) There should not be too many teaching aids. Too many teaching aids shall make the lesson burdensome and uninteresting. It shall also be an expensive method of teaching.

Previous Knowledge

This forms the plank of the introduction. It is on the basis of this knowledge that the teacher begins his lesson. He has to know what the boys already know.

The Lesson Plan

Introduction or preparation: The lesson starts at this stage. Introduction should be based on the following objectives

(1) To test the previous knowledge.

(2) To prepare proper and effective atmosphere for acquiring the new knowledge.

(3) To prepare the students to acquire the new knowledge.

Method of Introduction

There is no specific method or set pattern for introduction. The teacher may begin his lesson by presenting a picture, a chart or a model. He may also narrate a story.

Questioning. If the introduction is begun with questions, it should be remembered that the questions do not exceed three or four. These questions should be psychological and well-ordered. These questions should be based on the previous knowledge of the students. They should not be separate from each other but they should be inter-linked.

Statement of aim. After the introduction, the teacher should state the main aim of his lesson. He should tell the students what topic he is going to teach and with what objective in view.

This statement should be brief and in a simple language. It should enable to create the following 'We' in the students.

Presentation. Now the new lesson is presented. Attempt is made to correlate and coordinate the subject-matter with other topics of subjects while presenting the lesson. The pupil teacher may employ different methods and different teaching aids in order to present the subject-matter. In the training colleges, the questioning technique or narration technique is generally employed. Direct positive questions should not be used as far as possible.

Division in different units. In accordance with the convenience of the teacher, the students and the topic the teacher may divide the whole topic or lesson into different units.

Writing black-board substance. At the end of each unit, the substance of the topic taught should be put down on the black-board.

In different training institutions the use of the black-board is made in different ways. At some places only recapitulatory questions are put down on the black-board as a substance. At other places an attempt is made to develop the black-board substance alongwith the lesson. While the teaching is going on, the students are not allowed to copy out the substance. They write down the substance, after the presentation of the lesson has come to an end.

Recapitulation. The main aim of recapitulation is to ascertain and test the knowledge acquired by the students. It is also useful in testing the work of the teacher. Recapitulation should not take much time, it should finish in three or four questions.

Home Task or Home Work. The main aim of the home work is to develop the habit of self-study in the students and to enable them to make knowledge stable and permanent. It also broadens their outlook and knowledge.

While assigning the home work, the teacher should keep the interest, the aptitudes, individual differences, etc., of the students in mind.

Correction Work. The teacher should correct the home work of the students in their presence every day.

CIVICS LESSON PLAN NO. 1

N. A. S. Inter College, Aligarh

Day and Date: Monday, 6th September, 1999 Class- VI

Subject- Civics Period- 4th period

Topic- Functions of the Municipal Board Average age- 11 years.

Time- 35 minutes.

Name of the pupil-teacher- Rajendra Kumar Sharma.

General Aims

(1) To inculcate the spirit of ideal citizenship in the students.

(2) To teach them rights and duties of the citizens and the State.

(3) To teach them the lesson of self-control.

(4) To inculcate in them the sense of world brotherhood or world fraternity.

(5) To enable them to grow into useful citizens of the society.

(6) To create and develop in them an interest for the study of the Civics.

(7) To bring about the development of the traits of sympathy, sacrifice, co-operation and character in the students.

(8) To develop the powers of thinking, reasoning, imagination and decision making in the students.

(9) To develop scientific outlook in the students.

(10) To give the students an idea of social needs and requirements, and develop in them those social qualities that bring about social efficiency.

Specific Aims

To teach the students the functions of the Municipal Board.

Teaching Aids

(1) A picture showing a city without any provision of the roads, drains, bridges, etc. There is also dirt and filth scattered all around.

(2) A picture which shows a city with proper arrangement of the roads, drains, sanitation, etc.

(3) A picture depicting certain officers of the Municipal Board inspecting certain things.

(4) A chart that depicts the organisation of various social institutions.

Previous knowledge

The students are well aware of the life in the city and the administration of the civic or city life. They are also aware of the fact that Municipal Board arranges for every day sanitation and cleaning of the roads, etc. They have also seen and known the elections of the Municipal Board.

Introduction

Questions by the teacher

(1) Why do you clean your house?

Answer by the student ....

(2) Which is that organisation about whose election you have already read?

Answer by the student ....

(3) What are the functions of the Municipal Board?

Answer by the student ....

(4) What are the sources of income of Municipal Board?

Answer by the student ....

Statement of Aims

Today we shall study about the functions of the Municipal Board.

First Unit of the Lesson

Introduction or Presentation

(1) Why is the sanitation and cleanliness of your city necessary?

(2) What is the harm if the city is not cleaned?

(3) In the morning, every day, employees of which body carry out the sanitation and cleaning of the roads and the drains of your mohalla?

Statement of the Teacher

In the morning, we see certain persons doing the job of cleaning of the roads and the drains of the city. They are the persons appointed for the job by the Municipal Board. The first task of the Municipal Board is to keep the roads, drains and other places of the city neat and clean.

Demonstration of the Picture

Here the teacher shall show that picture of the city, where there is no arrangement of roads, drains, bridges, etc.

After showing the picture, the teacher shall ask :

(1) What do you see in this picture?

(2) Why no proper arrangement of the roads has been made here?

(3) Why is there no proper arrangement of the drains?

(4) Why does the dirty water flow here and there?

(5) How are the people moving about and going from one place to other?

(6) How are people crossing the river?

(7) What is the reason for all this mismanagement?

Statement of the Teacher

The roads of this city are broken. In the rainy season the water causes a lot of mud. Because there is no arrangement of drainage, the dirty water flows here and there and spoils the passage.

On every side we find dirt and insanitation. The main cause of all this mis-management is that no Municipal Board has been formed in this city. It is the Municipal Board which is responsible for looking after all these arrangements.

Now the teacher will show the other picture. After the teacher has shown the second picture, he shall put the following questions

(1) What is the difference between the first picture and this second picture?

(2) What is the condition of the roads in this picture?

(3) Why is dirty water not seen flowing on the roads?

(4) What is the arrangement of the markets?

Statement of the Teacher

Now we see that the main work of Municipal Boards is to build roads, arrange for drainage and markets, construct bridges and look after other conveniences of the civic life.

Black-board Substance

Then the teacher shall put down these various functions of the Municipal Board on the black-board in a legible, neat and good hand-writing.

Second Unit

Other functions of Municipal Board.

Presentation

The teacher shall put the following questions

(1) Who looks after the roads and the drains?

(2) Why is this arrangement made and care taken

(3) If the roads and the drains are not looked after, what harm shall it cause?

(4) Who organises fairs in your city?

(5) Who runs school in your city.

Statement of the Teacher

The main job of the Municipal Board is to build roads, look after the sanitation of the city, run primary schools, etc. If the Municipal Board does not look after the sanitation, filth is likely to cause several diseases. Officers of the Municipal Board are responsible for arranging and helping fairs in the city.

Demonstration of the Picture

After the teacher has shown the third picture to the students, he shall put the following questions :

The questions shall be put while the picture is before the eyes of the students.

The teacher shall ask –

(1) What do you see in the picture?

(2) Who looks after the roads and the drains of the city?

(3) Who appoints these officials?

(4) Which body organises the exhibitions?

(5) Officials of which body carry out innoculation when any epidemic breaks out?

Statement of the Teacher

Now we see that Municipal Board is responsible for the sanitation of the city, building good roads, organising fairs and exhibitions and deputing its officials to innoculate people when an epidemic breaks out.

Primary schools are also run by the Municipal Board.

Black-board Substance

The teacher shall put down his aforesaid statement in short on the black-board in a good hand-writing. Only functions of the Municipal Board should be to put down on the black-board.

Recapitulation: In order to test the knowledge of the subject taught in the class room, the teacher shall put down the following questions to the students :

(1) Which is that body which looks after the sanitation of your city?

(2) What are the various functions of that body in regard to sanitation?

(3) What are the various duties that this body discharges?

(4) Give a description of all these things in detail?

Home Work: The student should be asked to write at home and bring to the class room the various functions of the Municipal Board.

LESSON PLAN NO. 2

Raghunath Girls Inter College, Lucknow

Day and date: Tuesday, 17th September 1999

Class IX

Subject: Civics

Period V

Topic: Various social evils and the ways to eradicate them

Average age: 15 years.

Time: 40 minutes.

Name of the pupil-teacher: Mrs. Urmila Sharma

General Aims

(1) To encourage the student to grow into an ideal citizen.

(2) To mould the students into useful members of the society and to develop such qualities in them, as may bring about social good.

(3) To develop mental faculties like thinking, reasoning, judgment, etc.

(4) To develop the sentiments of Nationalism and Internationalism and to divert them towards the ideal of 'World brotherhood'.

(5) To develop respect for moral values in the student.

Specific Aims

To acquaint the students with the social evils and to tell them the ways and means of eradicating the social evils.

Teaching Aids

Two charts, in one there should be a list and description of the social evils and in the other there should be a list of the ways and means of eradicating those social evils: The whole description should be depicted with the help of pictures as far as possible.

Previous Knowledge

Students live in the society. They are well acquainted with various social actions and inter-actions. They are acquainted with the customs and traditions of the society.

Introduction

At first the teacher shall present the first chart before the students. This chart shall describe various social evils with the help of the pictures. Then he shall put down the following questions and the students shall come out with answers.

Question 1. What do you see in the first part of the picture? (The teacher shall point out towards a particular picture with the help of the pointer).

Answer of the student. People are drinking wine in the temple.

Question 2. What do you see in the other part of the picture?

Answer by the student. Living women are being burnt in the fire.

Question 3. What effect these scenes that you see in the picture, have on the society at large? How can they be removed from society

Answer ....

Presentation of the Aims. Today we shall read about the social evils and the ways and the means to eradicate them.

Presentation

Question 1. At what stage people are married in your society?

Answer ....

Question 2. What is the age fixed for the marriage of a boy and the marriage of a girl respectively.

Answer ....

Question 3. What should be the proportion in the age of the husband and the wife?

Answer ....

Question 4. Is there difference of only 5 to 6 years between the boy and the girl at the time of marriage?

Answer ....

Question 5. When there is difference of 20 to 25 years of age between the husband and the wife, what shall it be called?

Answer ....

Statement of the teacher. When there is a difference of 20 to 25 years of age between the husband and the wife, then it is called an ill-matched marriage. It is a social evil.

Question 6. What are the various social evils on which people spend a good deal of money?

Answer ....

Statement of the teacher. In our society people spend a good deal of money on wine, gambling, cinema-going, etc.

Note. After having made this statement, the teacher shall again put the following Questions.

Question 1. In the city, at what age generally boys and girls are married?

Answer ....

Question 2. What are the various problems of the Hindu society?

Answer ....

Question 3. Which problem is very important in Hindu society?

Answer ....

Question 4. What treatment is given out to women after the death of their husbands?

Answer ....

Question 5. Why are women burnt in the fire or burn themselves on the pyre?

Answer ....

Question 6. Why has this evil custom been removed

Answer ....

Question 7. What is the condition of the woman after the death of her husband

Answer ....

Question 8. What ways have been found out for such widows?

Answer ....

Question 9. Which of the two men or women is considered to be inferior in your society?

Answer ....

Question 10. Why is the woman considered inferior to man in Hindu society?

Answer ....

Statement of the teacher. In our society, ill-matched marriages and child marriages are two great social evils and problems. Other than these social evils, we have drinking, gambling, lack of widow re-marriage, sati, thinking women to be inferior, etc, as social evils and problems. Dowry system is the greatest social evil of the present-day society.

Ways to Eradicate the Social Evils

The teacher shall put the following Questions

Question 1. How can Sati system be removed?

Answer ....

Question 2. How can child-marriage be stopped in villages?

Answer ....

Question 3. How can social problems like dowry system, ill-matched marriages, stigma on widow re-marriage, etc., be solved?

Answer ....

Question 4. How can the status of the women in society be improved?

Answer ....

Question 5. How can social evils like drinking, gambling, etc., be done away with?

Answer ....

Question 6. Suggest the ways to remove the dowry system?

Answer ....

Statement of the teacher. The Government should try to frame such strict laws that people may not take to Sati, gambling, etc.

Law should also be framed to make ill-matched marriage an offence.

Such exhibitions and fairs should be arranged through which the people of the rural area may be acquainted with evil effects of these social evils.

Heavy duty should be imposed on intoxicants.

Dowry system should also be strictly imposed by law. Government have already banned it, but stricter enforcement of this measure is needed.

In order to improve the lot of the women, they should be given equal rights as are available to men. They should have freedom to take part in various aspects of social life. Widow re-marriage shall be a great boon in this direction.

Demonstration of the picture- Now the teacher shall show the other chart which contains the pictures of social reforms.

Black-board substance or writing substance on the Black-board. The teacher shall put down the following things on the black-board

Social problems or social evils. Problems of (i) Widow re-marriage, (ii) Child marriage, (iii) Ill-matched marriages, (iv) Low status of woman in the society, (v) Drinking, (vi) Gambling, (vii) Dowry system, (viii) Purdah system, etc.

Ways to remove the social evils. (i)To ban dowry system by law. (ii) To have strict control over gambling and drinking, to organise exhibitions and lectures, etc. (iii) To acquaint the village people with the results of these social evils. (iv) To make arrangement for the education of the woman. (v) To give equal rights to woman. (vi) To explain to people the importance of the woman in society.

It is possible to eradicate the social evils of ill-matched marriages only when the people of the rural areas are educated and conscious of the social evils of these things.

Recapitulation. The teacher may bring about the recapitulation with the help of the following:

Question 1. What are the various evils and main problems?

Answer ....

Question 2. How can these problems be solved and evils removed?

Answer ....

Home work

The students shall be asked to write an essay on the evils of the Indian society and the ways and means to remove them.

The teacher shall correct homework in the class room.

LESSON PLAN NO. 3

Govt. Higher Secondary School, Allahabad

Day and date- Wednesday, 8th September 1999

Class- III

Subject- Civics

Period- III

Topic- Regulated life

Average age- 8 Years.

Time- 35 minutes

Name of the pupil-teacher- Ravindra Sharma.

General Aims

(1) To teach the students about citizenship.

(2) To develop various social qualities in the students.

(3) To bring about the intellectual development of the students.

(4) To inculcate in the students such qualities that shall be helpful for the society in future and shall bring about the betterment of the human society at large.

(5) To teach the students the importance of good health and the merits and advantages of it.

Specific Aims

(1) To acquaint the students with the importance of regulated life.

(2) To acquaint them with the advantages and merits of a regulated life.

(3) To tell them to lead a regulated life.

Teaching Aids

A chart in which regulated life has been depicted through pictures.

Knowledge Assumed

The students are aware of regulated life. They lead the life according to the instruction of their guardians. In the morning the parents ask the children to get up and wash their hands and face.

Introduction. It may be carried out with the help of the following Questions.

Question 1. Children, at what time do you get up?

Answer ....

Question 2. What do you do after you get up?

Answer ....

Question 3. What is your routine of life for the whole day?

Answer ....

Statement of the teacher. Today we shall study as to what should be the routine of our every day life. We shall also study the various advantages of such a regulated life.

Statement of the teacher. Every day you should get up early in the morning. After attending to every-day needs, you should go to the park for walk. You should come back home before sunrise. After having a light refreshment you should read your lesson. The lesson should be read with interest and learnt properly.

When the mother calls, you should go for a bath and then sit down to eat, according to the orders of your mother. After taking food, you should go to the school at the proper time. When the school closes, you should come back home early and at the proper time. Then you should wash your hands and face and take some light refreshment. Now you should go out for games.

It is not proper to consume a good deal of time in games. It is better to return home before sunset. Now again hands and face should be washed. Good food should be taken. After taking food you should again sit down to study. At 9'o clock or 10 o'clock you should go to bed.

All the work should be carried out in a regulated manner.

Advantages and importance. Regulated life has the following advantages

(1) It keeps the body healthy and free from diseases.

(2) It also keeps the body smart and agile. When the body is healthy, the child feels interested in study and he also remains cheerful. Cheerfulness or happiness is very helpful for the mind.

Black-board Work

The teacher should demonstrate the chart and put the following questions to the students.

Questions 1. What do you see in the first part of the picture?

Answer ....

Question 2. What is the child doing?

Answer ....

Question 3. After having washed his hands and face, what is the child doing now?

Answer ....

Question 4. How is the child taking his food?

Answer ....

Question 5. What is he doing after taking his food? What is he preparing for?

Answer ....

Question 6. Where is the child going after being free from the school.

Answer ....

Question 7. What is he doing after coming back home from the school?

Answer ....

Question 8. Where is the child going, with the bat in his hand?

Answer ....

Question 9. After playing, what does he do after coming home?

Answer ....

Question 10. After reading, what does he do after putting the light out?

Answer ....

Now the teacher points out to the other part of the chart and puts the following questions to the students.

Question 1. What effect has the getting up in time on the health of the child? How is the child looking?

Answer ....

Question 2. Why is he looking here and there while he is reading?

Answer ....

Question 3. Why does he look cheerful all the time?

Answer ....

Question 4. How are his clothes?

Answer ....

Question 5. Why are his parents showing love to him?

Answer ....

Black-Board work

Regulated life

(1) You should get up in the morning at the right time.

(2) After having washed your hands and face you should go out for a walk.

(3) Then you should have light refreshment and sit down for reading.

(4) After taking bath, you should take your food at the right time and go to school at the proper time.

(5) After coming back from the school, you should have light refreshment and go out for playing.

(6) After returning from the play-field, you should take your food and sit down to study.

(7) Children, you should go to bed at the proper time.

Advantages

(1) It keeps the body healthy.

(2) There is cheerfulness all the time.

(3) There is agility and smartness in the body.

(4) You feel interested in doing work and reading.

(5) Then all elder people love you.

Recapitulation

It may be carried out with the help of the following questions

Question 1. What sort of regulated life should you lead?

Answer ....

Question 2. What are the advantages of such a life.

Answer ....

Home Task

Children shall not be given any written home work. They shall only be asked to lead such a life in practical manner. The direction should be inspiring and encouraging.

LESSON PLAN NO. 4

S. S. D. Higher Secondary School, Agra

Day and date- Thursday, 9th September 1999

Class- VIII

Subject— Civics.

Period- II

Topic- India and the world

Average age- 12 years.

Sub-unit- The United Nations

Time- 35 minutes

Name of the pupil-teacher- Rachana Sharma.

General Aims

1. To enable the pupils to learn about the origin of the various organs of U.N.O.

2. To enable the pupils to know the functions of the various organs of U.N.O.

3. To enable the pupils to know how U.N.O. is trying to solve the problems of international peace.

Specific Aims

1. To enable the pupils to develop the following understanding

(i) The U.N. is the latest and most ambitious human attempt to break down the barriers separating peoples and nations and to build a peaceful and just international community.

(ii) The United Nations seek to maintain justice and friendly relations based on equal rights of all peoples.

(iii) Peace is possible only through cooperation and mutual understanding among peoples.

(iv) A great moral force in the world, the U.N. wields a tremendous influence through the force of public opinion, though it has limited power.

2. To develop an international outlook in the pupils.

3. To develop the following skills in the pupils

(i) Preparing charts regarding the composition and organisation of U.N.O. and its various organs.

(ii) Preparing a list of members of the U.N. and keeping it up-to-date.

Teaching Aids

1. A map of the world showing the location of the Headquarters of the U.N.O.

2. A map of the world showing the Headquarters of the U.N.O. and places of conflict in the world.

Knowledge Assumed

The pupils are familiar with the need for cooperation among nations and the work of UNICEF, WHO, UNESCO, etc.

Previous Knowledge Test

In order to test the previous knowledge of the pupils, the teacher will ask the questions

1. Why is there need of cooperation among nations of the world?
2. What does UNICEF stand for? What are its functions?
3. What does UNESCO stand for? What are its functions?
4. What do you know about U.N.O. and its main organs?

The pupils will not be able to give a comprehensive answer. The teacher will announce the aim.

Presentation

Statement of the teacher- Today, we shall learn in detail about U.N. and see how it has resolved crises in many situations in the world and helped in the maintenance of peace.

Black Board work

Matter

The United Nations Organisation is an association of 149 nations which have pledged themselves for the maintenance of international peace and security. The states agree to cooperate in promoting such political, economic and social conditions as may facilitate these objectives.

Questions by the teacher

Q. What is U.N.O.?

Answer ....

Many attempts for maintenance of international peace and security had been made in the nineteenth century. The first constructive effort towards the establishment of a permanent international organisation for peace was the League of Nations which did not last long. The need for the United Nations was strongly felt during the Second World War. Devastation and horrors of the war intensified the longing for peace and security. Therefore, as a result of the cooperation of the Allied Powers, a series of war time conferences were held.

Question by the teacher

Q. What do you know about the origin of the U.N.O.?

Answer ....

The teacher will show San Francisco on the map.

Teaching Material

The United Nations Organisation was born on 25th June, 1945 at San Francisco when 111 articles of the charter were adopted by 51 countries as a symbol of international cooperation and understanding for a better world. The name of the United Nations was given at the instance of President Roosevelt. The Organisation actually came into being on 24th October, 1945.

Following are the aims of the U.N.O.

1. To maintain international peace and security.
2. To develop a spirit of cooperation and friendly relations among the nations of the world.
3. To promote and encourage respect for human rights and for fundamental freedom.

4. To solve international problems of economic, social, cultural and humanitarian character.

5. To employ international machinery for the promotion of economic and social advancement of all peoples.

The purposes of the U.N.O. can thus be divided into four groups, viz., security, justice, welfare and human rights.

Question by the Teacher

Q. What are the aims and purpose of U.N.O ?

Answer ....

Section Revision

1. When was the U.N. born?
2. Who suggested the name of U.N.O.?
3. What are the main aims of U.N.O.?

Teaching Material

The main organs of the U.N. are

1. General Assembly, 2. Security Council, 3. Economic and Social Council, 4. Trusteeship Council. 5. International Court of Justice, 6. Secretariat.

1. *General Assembly.* It is the main body of the U.N. It consists of all the member nations, each nation can send five representatives, though each has only one vote. General Assembly meets regularly once a year. Special and emergency sessions can also be summoned. The assembly discusses ways and means of preserving peace, disarmament, peaceful uses of atomic energy, economic development and social progress, etc.

2. *Security Council.* The Council consists of five permanent members, viz., People's Republic of China, France, the U.S.S.R., the U.K., the U.S.A. and ten non-permanent members, who are elected by the General Assembly for two years from among the member states. It is the executive body of the U.N., that is mainly responsible for maintaining international peace. It is in session all the year round, and can meet at 24 hours notice.

3. ***Economic and Social Council.*** It consists of 54 members elected by the General Assembly. The members are elected for a term of three years. The U.N, tries to achieve international cooperation through this Council by solving international problems of economic, social, cultural, and humanitarian character and by promoting respect for human rights and fundamental freedoms for all without distinction of race, sex, language or religion. It meets at least thrice a year.

4. ***Trusteeship Council.*** It consists of 14 member-nations. It is incharge of all the territories which were administered before World War II under the Mandate of the League of Nations. It seeks to ensure the political; economic, social and educational advancement of the people living in Trust Territories such as. East New Guinea, Marshal Islands, Carolinae, Marianas.

5. ***International Court of Justice.*** Serving as a principal judicial organ of the U.N., it consists of fifteen judges elected for a nine-year term by the Security Council and General Assembly; five judges retiring every three years. It gives advisory opinion on legal matters to the various organs and specialised agencies of the U.N.

6. ***Secretariat.*** To serve the U.N. and its organs, there is a working force of over 10,000 men and women of U.N. member-nations employed in the Secretariat. The Secretariat is headed by the Secretary-General, Chief Executive Officer of the United Nations, appointed by the General Assembly upon the recommendation of the Security Council.

Question by the Teacher

Q. 1. Which are the main organs of the U. N.?

Answer ....

Q. 2. What are their functions?

Answer ....

Sectional Revision

1. Name the main organs of U.N.
2. Who heads the Secretariat?
3. What is the function of international Court of Justice?

Teaching Material

The greatest good U.N. has done is that it has provided a forum where nations can meet and discuss their conflicting claims, and it can use its influence for moderation and conciliation. It serves as a great deterrent to the aggressor. It has played the part of international policemen. It has intervened successfully and has been able to exert its moderating influence in a number of cases.

Achievements of U.N.

1. It mediated in Indonesia. The Dutch forces were withdrawn and Republic of United States of Indonesia was established.
2. It ordered a ceasefire in 1949 when war was going on between India and Pakistan on Kashmir border.
3. It stopped aggression in South Korea, and drove away the aggressors.
4. The United Nations Political Committee unanimously approved a resolution envisaging a concrete plan for world cooperation to develop atomic energy for peaceful uses; the International Atomic Energy Commission has been set up.
5. It helped in ending colonialism in Indonesia, Tunisia, Morocco, Algeria and Cyprus, etc., and helped in the birth of new independent nations.
6. The Cuban crisis of October 1962 was resolved by the intervention of the U.N. Secretary-General U. Thant
7. It intervened in the West Asian War of June, 1961 and brought about a ceasefire.

8. It called upon India and Pakistan to agree to a ceasefire in Kashmir on 23rd Sept., 1965.

9. The United Nations met in an Emergency Session in 1971 to discuss the Indo-Pak conflict in Bangladesh.

10. In November 1974 it averted the threat of immediate war between Turkey and Greece.

Question by the Teacher

Q. 1. What are the achievements of U.N. in the political field?

Answer ....

Full use will be made of the world map for showing places of conflict.

Sectional Revision

1. Give an account of the achievements of U.N. in resolving the crises and in maintaining peace.

Recapitulation

1. Why was the need felt for U.N.?
2. Name the various organs of U.N.
3. What are the achievements of U.N. in the political field?

Black-board Summary

Birth of U.N. 25th June, 1945 at San Francisco, 111 articles of Charter adopted by 51 countries.

Main Purposes. Security, Justice, Welfare and Human Rights.

Main Organs. General Assembly, Security Council, the Economic and Social Council, Trusteeship Council, International Court of Justice, Secretariat.

Achievements. It stopped hostilities in Kashmir, Korea, Cuba, etc. It helped in ending colonialism in Indonesia, Tunisia, Morocco, Algeria and Cyprus, etc.

ACTIVITIES

1. With the help of students, the teacher can organise panel discussions and U.N. mock sessions on some issues before U.N.
2. The teacher can show the following films in the class- World Without End, A Garden We Planted Together, Three Promises.
3. Students may be encouraged to collect articles, photographs, pictures and clippings from newspapers and magazines for display on bulletin board, wall newspapers, etc.

15
The Curriculum

The term 'curriculum' is of Latin origin and it implies an athletic ground, thus indicating that curriculum is the ground through which the educand has to pass in order to reach a definite goal. In the past the term was taken to mean a collection of knowledge and skill. It did not then imply the educand's needs, but instead the knowledge and skills of the specialists working in different spheres. But the modern interpretation of the term is clarified by Bent and Kronenburg, who suggest that the curriculum is the organized form of subject matter, specially prepared to meet the requirements of children. Hence, now curriculum includes those experiences and activities which provide the student with the knowledge and the skills he will require in facing the various situations of real life. Obviously, the term 'curriculum' cannot be restricted to a list of books, because it must include other activities, the environment of the school and numerous other elements not taught by books. In the words of Bent and Kronenburg, "Curriculum, in its broadest sense, includes the complete school environment involving all the courses, activities, reading and association furnished to the pupils in the school."

The Definition

It will be easier to understand the concept of curriculum by glancing at a few definitions given as follows-

Curriculum is experience. In the words of Munroe, "Curriculum embodies all the experiences which are utilized by the school to attain the aims of education." Thus, the various subjects included for study in a curriculum are not intended merely for study or rote learning but to convey experiences of various kinds. The concept has been defined in more or less the same terms in the report of the

Secondary Education Commission in these words, "Curriculum does not mean only the academic subjects traditionally taught in the school, but it includes the totality of experiences that a pupil receives through the manifold activities that go on in the school, in the classroom, library, laboratory, workshop, playgrounds and in the numerous informal contacts between teachers and pupils." Another definition of curriculum as experience is provided by Crow and Crow, "The curriculum includes all the learner's experiences in or outside school that are included in a programme which has been devised to help him develop mentally, physically, emotionally, socially, spiritually and morally." It is obvious, then, that the aim of curriculum is to provide experience to the educand so that he may achieve complete development. By calling the curriculum an experience, the fact is made explicit that it includes not merely books but all those activities and relationships which are indulged in by the educand both inside and outside the school. Hence, the syllabi specified by the authority should not be taken to mean curriculum.

Curriculum is a means or tool. It is apparent from the foregoing definitions that curriculum is not an end in itself, but a means to an end, because it is created in order to achieve the aims of education. That is why one finds that different educationists have suggested different kinds of curricula to conform to the aims and objectives ascribed to education. Explaining the concept of curriculum as a tool of education, Cunningham writes, "The curriculum is the tool in the hands of the artist (the teacher) to mould his material (the pupil) according to his ideal (objective) in his studio (the school)." Here the educator is-compared to an artist and the curriculum as one of the instruments or tools used by him to develop the educand according to and in conformity with the aims of education. It is evident that the curriculum will change with every change in the aims of education.

Curriculum is environment. The most comprehensive definition of curriculum is given by those who conceive it to include the total environment of the school. In the words of H.L. Laswell, "The curriculum is made up of everything that surrounds the learner in all his working hours." In fact, the curriculum has been described as "the environment in motion." In modern times, this term is interpreted in this more liberal sense because there is no questioning the fact that the child's education is influenced by not only books but the playgrounds, library, laboratory, reading room, extra-curricular programmes, the educational environment, and a host of other factors. In the school both the educator and the educand are part of the curriculum because they are part of the environment, while in the family the child and his parents are part of the educational environment. Hence, the formation of the curriculum is not restricted to making a list of subjects or text-books but must include a complete definition of the total environment in which the child is expected to progress and achieve the goals of education.

Curriculum includes all activities. It is stated in the *Twenty-ninth Year Book of the National Society for the Study of Education,* U.S.A. that, "The curriculum may be defined as the totality of subject matter, activities and experiences which constitute a pupil's school life." Elaborating the same concept further, H.H. Horne says, "The curriculum is that which the pupil is taught. It involves more than the acts of learning and quiet study; it involves occupations, productions, achievement, exercise, activity." Pragmatists, too, have included the entire range of the educand's activities in the curriculum because according to them the child learns by doing.

In the light of the various definitions of curriculum given above, it is possible to arrive at a definition of the terms which includes all the points mentioned in these definitions. Briefly, the curriculum is the means of achieving the goals of education. It includes all these experiences, activities and environments which the educand receives during his educational career. Such a definition of curriculum comprehends the educand's entire life, a contention borne out by all modern educationists who believe that the child learns not only inside the school but also outside it, on the playground, at home, in society, in fact, everywhere. That is why there is nowadays so much insistence on the participation of the parents in the child's education and on not restricting the environment of the curriculum to the school environment, but taking it to mean every possible kind of environment encountered by the child. Besides, it includes all those activities which the child does, irrespective of the time and place of these activities. It also includes the entire range of experiences that the child has in the school, at home, in the world at large. Considered from this liberal standpoint, one finds that in preparing the curriculum one has a much wider background than would otherwise be possible.

Aims and Objectives

Clarifying the aims and objectives of curriculum it has been pointed out in the report of the Secondary Education Commission that, "The starting point for curricular reconstruction must therefore be the device to bridge the gulf between the school subjects and to enrich the varied activities that make up the warp and woof of life.." Hence, the curriculum should be so designed that it trains the educand to face the situations of real life, a curriculum can be said to have the following major objectives :

Synthesis of subject and life. The aim of the curriculum is to arrange and provide those subjects for an educand's study which will enable the educand to destroy any gulf between school life and life outside the school. The opinion of the Secondary Education Commission has already been quoted.

Complete development. The aim of the curriculum is to achieve the physical, mental, social, moral, religious, spiritual, in fact, complete development of the educand. Hence, while determining a curriculum it is essential to see whether it will make such a complete development possible.

Development of democratic values. In all democratic countries, the curriculum of education must aim to develop the democratic values of equality, liberty and fraternity, so that the educands may develop into the fine democratic citizens. But this development should not only aim at national benefit. The curriculum must also aim at introducing a spirit of internationalism in the educand.

Satisfaction of the educand's needs. In defining curriculum, many educationists have insisted that it must be designed to satisfy the needs and requirements of the educand. It is seen that one finds a great variety of interests, skills, abilities, attitudes, aptitudes, etc., among educands. A curriculum should be so designed as to satisfy the general and specific requirements of the educands.

Realization of values. One aim of education is development of character, and what is required for this is to create in the educand a faith in the various desirable values. Hence, one of the objectives of education is to create in the educand a definite realization of the prevailing system of values.

Development of knowledge. In its most common connotation, the term curriculum is taken to mean development of knowledge or acquisition of facts. And, very frequently, this is the aspect kept in mind while designing a curriculum. But it must be remembered that it is not the only objective, although it is the most fundamental objective of a curriculum.

Creation of a useful environment. Another objective of curriculum is to create an environment suitable to the educand. Primarily, the environment must assist the educand in achieving the maximum possible development of his faculties, abilities and capabilities.

Addition to knowledge. In the contemporary educational patterns, that curriculum is believed to be suitable which can create harmony, between the various branches of knowledge so that the educand's attitude should be comprehensive and complete, not one-sided.

Harmony between individual and society. In a democracy such social qualities as social skill, cooperation, the desire to be of service, sympathy, etc., are very significant because, without them, no society can continue to exist. On the other hand, development of the individual's own character and personality are also very important. Hence, the curriculum must create an environment and provide those books which enable the individual to achieve his own development at the same time as he learns these social qualities.

Relation with Syllabus

The relationship between curriculum and syllabus is made very clear by the foregoing description of the aims of curriculum. Curriculum is not merely syllabus, because the latter is only verbal, book-oriented and theoretical, while the former is not. Syllabus places more stress on learning and memory. On the other hand, the scope of the curriculum is much greater for it comprehends every aspect of the educand's life, seeks to satisfy all his requirements and to develop every aspect of his personality. Hence, the syllabus is part and parcel of the curriculum, but the two terms should not be treated as synonymous. In addition to the syllabus, the curriculum also includes various kinds of extra-curricular activities and all the various parts of the educational environment. Despite this, the syllabus is treated as the basis of curriculum in the school, although it is improper to restrict the curriculum in this manner.

The Bases

It is seen everywhere that the form of the curriculum undergoes a change whenever the aims of education are altered to suit changed conditions in society. For this reason, it is necessary to define the various bases of curriculum, of which the more important ones are the following:

Aims of education. One finds differences of curriculum according to the differing aims of education determined by the different philosophies of education such as idealism, realism, pragmatism, etc. If the aim of education is to bring about an industrial revolution then the curriculum will place more stress on industrial activity but if education seeks to build the character of the educand, the curriculum will naturally lay a heavy emphasis upon the study of those subjects which help in character formation. If the curriculum aims at preparing the educand for future life and enabling him to earn his livelihood, it must include those subjects which give the educand some professional skill.

Philosophy of education. Another basis of the formation of curriculum is the philosophy of education. Difference in philosophic concepts leads to changes in the curriculum. Philosophy considers such fundamental and profound questions as man's place in the universe, the aims of nature, the aims of society, the relationship between man and society, etc. In every philosophy the answer derived for these questions is different, and this difference lends colour to the curriculum.

Sociological basis. In recent times, the curriculum has always been profoundly influenced by the discoveries of the various social sciences. This constitutes the sociological basis of education.

Psychological basis. But the most important basis of curriculum formation is the psychological one. In modern times so much research has been conducted in the sphere of educational psychology that it has become an independent branch of psychology. These researches have had great impact on the shaping of curricula and this is only natural since the curriculum is only a means to the educand's development. Hence, it should be shaped by the psychology of the educand.

Curriculum Construction

Different educationists have expressed their own views about the fundamental principles of curriculum, the difference being created by their different philosophies of education. Briefly, the main principles of curriculum construction are the following:

Principle of utility. T. P. Nunn, the educationist, believes that principle of utility is the most important principle underlying the formation of a curriculum. He writes, "While the plain man generally likes his children to pick up some scraps of useless learning for purely decorative purposes, he requires, on the whole, that they shall be taught what will be useful to them in later life, and he is inclined to give `useful' a rather strict interpretation." As a general rule, parents are in favour of including all those subjects in the curriculum which are likely to prove useful for their child in his life and by means of which he can be made a responsible member of society.

Training in the proper pattern of conduct. According to Crow and Crow, the main principle underlying the construction of a curriculum is that through education the educand should be able to adopt the patterns of behaviour proper to different circumstances. Man is a social animal who has to constantly adapt himself to social environment. Therefore, education must aim at developing all those qualities in the educand which will facilitate this adaptation to the social milieu. The child is by nature self-centered, but education must teach him to attend to the needs and requirements of others besides himself: One criterion of an educated individual is that be should be able to adapt himself to different situations with which he is confronted. In this context, the term conduct must be understood in its widest sense. Only then can this principle of curriculum construction be properly understood. All our activities in social, economic, family, cultural environment constitute behaviour or conduct, and it is the function of education to teach us how to behave in different situations.

Synthesis of play and work. Of the various modern techniques of education, some try to educate through work and others through play. But a great majority of educationists agree that the curriculum should aim at achieving a balance between play and work. In other words, the work given to the educand should be performed in such a manner that the child may believe it to be play. There is difference between work and play. That is why parents want to engage the child in work instead of allowing him to play all the time, but the child is naturally inclined to spend his time in playing. Keeping this in view, T. P. Nunn has written, "The school should be thought of not as a knowledge monger's shop but a place where the young are disciplined in certain forms of activity. All subjects should be taught in the "play way", care being taken that the "way" leads continuously from the irresponsible frolic of childhood to the disciplined labours of manhood."

Synthesis of all activities of life. In framing a curriculum, attention should be paid to the inclusion, in it, of all the various activities of life, such as contemplation, learning, acquisition of various kinds of skills, etc. In the individual and social sphere of life, every individual has to perform a great variety of activities, and his success in life is determined by the success of all these activities. Hence, the curriculum should not neglect any form of activity related to any aspect of life. A curriculum constructed on this basis will be both comprehensive and closely related to life. In other words, it should include all the activities that the educand is likely to require in later life.

Principle of individual differences. Modern educational psychology has brought to light, and stresses the significance of individual differences that exist between one individual and another. It has been discovered that people differ in respect of their mental processes, interests, aptitudes, attitudes, abilities, skills, etc., and these differences are innate. All modern education is paidocentric, that is, it is centred around the child. Psychologists insist that the curriculum should be so designed as to provide an opportunity for complete and comprehensive development to widely differing individuals. One of the basic qualities of such a curriculum is flexibility, for it must be flexible in order to accommodate educands of low, average or high intelligence and ability, and to provide each one a chance to develop all these abilities to the greatest possible extent.

Constant development. Another basis for curriculum construction is the principle of a dynamic curriculum based on the realization that no curriculum can prove adequate for all times and in all places. For this reason the curriculum should be flexible and changeable. This is all the more true in the modern context when new discoveries in the various branches of science are taking place every day. Hence, it becomes necessary to reshape the curriculum fairly frequently in order to incorporate the latest developments.

Creative training. Another important principle of curriculum construction is that of creative training. Raymont has correctly stated that a curriculum appropriate for the needs of today and the future must definitely have a positive bias towards creative subjects. And, one of the aims of education is to develop the creative faculty of the educand. All that is finest in human culture is the creation of man's creative abilities. Children differ from each other in respect of this ability. Hence, in framing a curriculum attention must be paid to the fact that it should encourage each educand to develop his creative ability as far as it is possible.

Variety. Variety is another important principle of curriculum construction. The innate complexity of man and the many facets of his personality make it necessary that the curriculum should be varied, because no one kind of curriculum can develop all the faculties of an individual. Hence, at every level the curriculum must have variety. It will, on the one hand, provide an opportunity for developing the different faculties of the educand, while, on the other, it will retain his interest in education.

Education for leisure. One of the objectives ascribed to education is training for leisure, because it is believed that education is not merely for employment or work. Hence, it is desirable that the curriculum should also include a training in those activities which will make the individual's leisure more pleasurable. A great variety of social, artistic and sporting activities can be included in this kind of training. Besides, educands should be encouraged to foster some or the other hobby so that they can put their leisure to constructive and pleasant use.

10. **Related to community life-** Curriculum can also be based on the principle that school and community life must be intimately related to each other. One cannot forget that the school is only a miniature form of community. Hence, the school curriculum should include all those activities which are performed by members of the larger community outside the boundaries of the school. This will help in evolving social qualities of the individual, in developing the

social aspect of his personality and finally helping his final adaptation to the social environment into which he must ultimately go.

Evolution of democratic values. The construction of a curriculum in a democratic society is conditioned by the need to develop democratic qualities in the individual. The curriculum should be so designed that it develops democratic thinking and creates a positive faith in democratic values. The programme devised in the college should lead to the development of the individual and social qualities in the educand so that he may be able to participate usefully and successfully in democratic life. In all the democratic societies of the world, this is the chief consideration in shaping the curricula for primary, secondary and higher education.

It is evident from the foregoing account of the various bases of curriculum construction that this should be duly conditioned by careful thinking on all aspects- individual and social, variety, play and work, earning of livelihood, leisure, etc.

The Importance

The following advantages are derived when the curriculum is constructed for various levels of education: -

Achievement of educational aims. The curriculum is constructed carefully in order to achieve the aims set for education, and therefore its advantage is that it helps in achieving these aims. In the absence of a curriculum it would be impossible to do anything systematically.

Limits of teaching and learning. In order, to implement the educational programmes properly in different schools, it is necessary to determine in advance the body of knowledge to be acquired by the educands at different levels of education, and also the amount of teaching to be done by the educators. This can only be fixed on the basis of the curriculum. It helps in determining the work of the educator as well as that of the educand.

Dissemination of knowledge. The aim of education is the dissemination of knowledge, and this is also the aim of the curriculum.

By studying the various subjects laid down in the curriculum, the educand acquires a quantity of knowledge in conformity with his abilities and level of intelligence. Different kinds of curricula are constructed for imparting education at different stages in the child's mental development.

Development of character. The curriculum of contemporary education aims not only at the dissemination of knowledge, but also at the development and formation of character because the child is kept in a social environment which encourages the development of all humane qualities in him. This improves the child's conduct and leads to development of character.

Development of personality. The various aspects of the educand's personality undergo change and development when he studies the various subjects prescribed in the curriculum, acquires different kinds of experience and adjust or adapts to different sets of circumstances.

Development of citizenship. In almost all modern States, development of citizenship is considered to be one of the major responsibilities of education, and the curriculum is designed with this end in view.

Discoveries and research. At the highest level of education, the curriculum is designed to encourage research and make inventions.

The Stages

Normally speaking we have five stages of education, namely, (1) Pre-primary, (2) Primary, (3) Junior High School, (4) Secondary, (5) University.

Syllabus or Curriculum at the Pre-primary and Primary Stage of Education. This is the stage of the children between the age of 4 to 11 years. Their education runs up to Class V At this stage of education the main aim is to develop the basic qualities of human life in the students. The syllabus of Civics for this stage of education should be of an elementary nature. It should be based on certain elementary principles of formation of good habits and imparting knowledge of necessary requirements of life.

Syllabus at the Junior High School Stage of Education. Here the course is of three years. The aim of education is to bring about the development of the physical and mental faculties of the students. As there is a tendency to acquire knowledge and make discoveries about things in the students, an attempt is made to integrate the teaching of Civics with the teaching of other subjects. Attempt is also made to teach the practical aspect of the Civics. The principles of Civics can very well be applied in the school life. The students can be shown the working of the theory at this stage in the world outside the school. In fact, the real aim of teaching Civics is to help the students to understand the elements of their social atmosphere, local life and the political and cultural aspect of the society. The syllabus of the Junior High Schools in Uttar Pradesh is as given below :

Syllabus for Class VI

We have the following things in the syllabus:

(i) The structure of the local administration- (a) towns, and (b) districts.

(ii) Organisation and functions of the Gram Sabhas and Gram Panchayats, their problems and the solutions of those problems.

(iii) Organisation and functions of the Municipalities and Zila Parishads.

(iv) National and local festivals.

Practical Work. Besides theoretical knowledge, the students are also expected to do the practical work. It includes the following:

(i) Organisation of the social service in the village or the town, sanitation and health of the town, drinking water, roads and measures for preventing the spread of diseases.

(ii) Celebration of national and local festivals and functions in the schools.

(iii) Celebration of the days of national importance such as Republic Day, Independence day, Gandhi Jayanti, Nehru Birthday, etc.

Syllabus for Class VII

It includes the theoretical knowledge of the following:

(i) The study of the working of the following :

(a) Governor, (b) Cabinet, and (c) Legislature.

(ii) Study of the structure of the administration of various States of India, with special reference to Uttar Pradesh.

(iii) Elections and franchise.

(iv) Structure of the judiciary in the court with special study of the following:

(a) Supreme Court, (b) High Court, and (c) Other subordinate courts.

(v) Problems of the social life of the country such as educational problems.

(vi) Problems of untouchability, poverty, indebtedness, agricultural problems, economic problems and other social problems.

Practical work. The theoretical knowledge of the students has to be given a practical shape. It can be done by employing the following measures:

(i) Continuance of the work started in class VI.

(ii) Practising the election system in the various bodies of the schools and the Unions.

(iii) Practising the principles of co-operation in the schools. This may be done by organising co-operative stores in the schools.

(iv) The democratic way of life may be practised in schools. Various committees of the students may be formed for the organisation and arrangement of various activities in the schools.

(v) Newspaper may be read collectively. A student may read the paper and others may listen to it.

(vi) Lectures on important topics may be arranged and organised.

Syllabus for Class VIII

The theoretical aspect of the syllabus includes the following:

(i) Study of the structure of administration of the Central Government of the Indian Republic.

(ii) Study of the political problems and the working of the political parties.

(iii) Study of the following organs of the Government of India- (a) President, (b) Cabinet, and (c) Parliament.

(iv) The following agencies and organisations of international importance may be studied with reference to India:

(a) United Nations Organisation

(b) United Nations Organisation and its various agencies and branches.

(v) Study of the influence of great men on the society, such as, Mahatma Gandhi, Rabindra Nath Tagore, Jawahar Lal Nehru, Sri Aurobindo Ghosh, etc.

(vi) Impact of scientific inventions and discoveries on the life of the society.

(vii) Impact of industrialization on society and various other problems.

Practical work. In this class also the theoretical' knowledge of the students has to be given a practical shape. It can be done by taking up the following activities:

(i) Continuance of the practical work done in the previous classes. An attempt should be made to improve it.

(ii) Study Groups should be organised. The working of the Parliamentary Government may be taught by organising School Parliament or such other activities.

(iii) An attempt should be made to help the expansion of education.

By casting a glance at the above syllabus., it becomes clear that at this stage of education an attempt is made to acquaint the students with the various political, social, religious and cultural problems of the society. The students are also taught to play their part in the solution of these problems.

Syllabus at the Secondary Stage of Education

When the student reaches this stage of education his mental powers such as imagination, reasoning; power of determination, etc, have developed. They have learnt the art of shouldering the responsibilities. They try to understand various social, political, religious and cultural problems. Hence, the syllabus at this stage of education should be scientific and properly organised. It should be competent to develop the students into ideal citizens of democratic republic.

Aims and Objectives of Teaching Civics at the Secondary Stage of Education

This stage of education includes four classes, IX, X, XI and XII. The teaching of civics should aim at the following:

(1) To develop the spirit of sacrifice, co-operation, love, etc, among the students so that they may try to lead the life of an ideal citizen.

(2) The students should be acquainted with the democratic system of government of the State. This shall encourage them to take interest in the working of the government.

(3) The student should be given an idea of the complex structure of the society and various social problems. They should be given an opportunity to observe various events and objects. That will develop the spirit of patriotism in them. This patriotism and nationalism shall be in co-existence with internationalism.

(4) By practising it, on a miniature stage, in the school, the students should be given a practical idea of the government.

(5) An attempt should be made to acquaint the students with the problems of the country, Traits of national consciousness, emotional integration, co-operation, equality etc. should be developed in them.

Syllabus at the First Two Years of Secondary Stage of Education.

At this stage of education there shall be two papers of civics. The syllabus of both these papers shall be as given below:

First paper. Principles and theory of Civics. This paper shall include the following:

(i) ***Citizenship.*** Meaning, how is it acquired and how is it lost. Rights and duties of a citizen, obstacles in the path of an ideal citizenship.

(ii) ***Individual society and associations.*** Its various kinds.

(iii) ***States.*** Relationship of the citizen with the State, functions of the State, etc.

(iv) ***Types of the Government.*** Their definitions:

(v) ***Various organs of the Government and their organisation.*** Legislature, Executive and Judiciary.

(vi) ***Law and Liberty.***

Second paper. This paper shall deal with citizenship and administration. It shall include the following:

(i) *Fundamental rights of the citizen under the 'Constitution.*

(ii) *State Government-* Their structure and relationship with the Central Government.

(iii) *Administration of the districts of the States-* District and Divisional Officers and their powers and duties.

(iv) *Local, administration-* Organisation and functions of the local bodies, Municipalities, Zila Parishad, their organisation and functions.

(v) *Rural administration-* This is administration of the village. Gram Panchayats, Gram Sabhas, etc., their organisation and functions

Syllabus for the Last Two Years of Secondary Education

According to the prospectus of the Board of High School, and Intermediation, classes shall include the following

First paper. Principles of Civic.

(i) ***Introductory.*** Its meaning, subject, its scope and its relation with other social sciences. Society, state and different types of communities.

(ii) ***State and individual.*** Sovereignty, law, freedom and equality and rights.

(iii) ***Origin of state theory.***

(iv) ***Functions of a state.*** Meaning of a welfare state

(v) ***Types of administration Constitutions.*** Their types and principles of their classifications.

(a) ***Legislative-voters.*** political organisations and public opinion, bicameral legislatures.

(b) ***Executive.*** Different forms and ways of appointment, relation with legislature.

(c) ***Judiciary-*** Appointment and its functions. Functions and importance of the modern judiciary.

(vi) ***Citizenship.*** Meaning, how to acquire citizenship, its rights and duties, hurdles in the functioning of ideal citizenship.

(vii) ***Ideals of civil life.*** Patriotism, Nationality, Internationalism, World Government.

Second Paper. Indian Administration and Civic life. Indian Union and its constitution. Constitution of Union Government and its functions :

(i) ***Union Executive. (1)*** President- Appointment, rights and functions, (2) Cabinet- Appointment and functions.

(ii) ***Union Legislature.*** Parliament, Rajya Sabha, Lok Sabha formation and rights.

(iii) ***Relation between the two houses and the Executive.*** Formation of State governments and their functioning, Centrally administered territories also included- Administrative position and study of North-East 'border states and Nagaland inclusive of Centrally administered areas.

(iv) ***Executives of States.*** Appointment, rights and functions.

(v) ***Legislatures of States.*** Legislative Assemblies-Organisation and rights.

(vi) ***Legislative Council.*** Organisation and Rights-Relation between the two houses and Executive

(vii) ***Indian Judiciary.*** Supreme Court and its importance.

Judicial System in UP

(viii) ***Public Services in India-*** Their importance, and their work and Public Service Commissions, Local self-government and its importance

(a) Municipalities, Corporations and Zila Parishads.

(b) Kshetra Samitis, Gaon Sabhas, Panchayat and Panchayti Adalat.

(c) Co-operative societies and community development schemes.

(ix) ***Movements for religious and social reformations in India-*** Their effect on political and national life of the country.

(x) ***National movement.*** Performance of the Indian National Congress and its importance.

(xi) ***Sectarian and communal movements-*** Political organisations in the country.

(xii) ***Indian economic life-*** (a) Farmer- His problems and rural life, (b) Industry and urban life, (c) Need of planned financial set up, (d) Programme of national plans.

(xiii) ***India and the world -*** As a member of the Commonwealth and its place in it as a member of the UNO.

(xiv) ***India and Asian Countries-*** Particularly in relation with the Peoples Republic of China and Pakistan.

Patel Committee Recommendations

Patel Committee has recommended that a general broad-based education be provided upto the end of the stage of compulsory education, so that children leaving school should have acquired a knowledge of our heritage and culture and are enabled to exercise their rights as citizens in a responsible manner. The Committee feels that while in classes VIII, IX and X, there should be general broad-based education, provision must be made for developing any special interests or talents in at least one area, outside the broad framework of general education.

The Committee has recommended that the content of courses of individual subjects of learning, must be designed so as to keep the quantum of knowledge to the minimum essential for the understanding of the subject.

The Syllabus

Class VI. Our Civic Community

1. Development of the Community: Scheme-Cooperatives-community development.

2. Local Government Rural: need- structure and functions.

3. Local Government Urban: structure and functions.

4. District Administration: Law and Order- civic amenities.

5. Preservation of property of the community: Public property, preservation- historical monuments.

6. Project Work: opportunities to develop abilities which are essential for any active citizen in India- problems.

Class VII. Our Constitution

1. Chief Features of Our Constitution- Basic Principles, National Government States governments- rights- duties- directive principles- national symbols.

2. Law-Making Process: Parliament- State legislature, How Laws are made.

3. Executing Laws: President- Prime Minister and the council of ministers, Governor- Chief Minister and-the council of ministers, public services.

4. Interpreting Law: Supreme Court, High Courts and subordinate courts.

5. Project Work.

Class VIII- Independent India- Achievements and Challenge

1. Our National Goals: Democracy- Socialism and Secularism, International Cooperation.

2. Strengthening our Democracy: citizenship in a democracy- literacy in India.
3. Social and Economic Reconstruction: poverty- population- unemployment- casteism.
4. Five Year Plans- Achievements and Failures, Agriculture, Industries- Rural Life.
5. Defence of the Country: Armed Forces- Territorial Army- Border Security Forces- N.C.C, A.C.C., citizens and defence.
6. India and the World: Need for cooperation- co-existence, the United Nations.
7. Project Work.

QUESTIONS

1. What is curriculum? Discuss its aims, objectives, bases and principles.
2. What share would you give to Civics in the Junior and Senior High School syllabus? Draw up briefly a syllabus for the same.
3. Give a critical estimate of the Syllabus in Civics for High School classes.

16

Correlation with Other Subjects

"No subject is ever well understood and no art is intelligently practised, if the light which the other studies are able to throw upon it is deliberately shut out." Education is a coordinated process. Teaching of various subjects is correlated. Herbert first conceived the idea of correlating the teaching of various subjects. Later on Zillar made this theory of correlation more elaborate. Then De Garmo and John Dewey laid stress on the integration in the teaching of various subjects. Today correlating the teaching of Civics is considered essential.

Kinds of Correlation and Coordination

(1) ***Vertical correlation:*** In vertical correlation an attempt is made to correlate the teaching of the various divisions of a subject. An attempt is also made to make the subject taught in the lower classes useful for the teaching of the same subject in the higher classes.

(2) ***Horizontal correlation:*** In horizontal correlation an attempt is made to coordinate the teaching of various subjects. This is done by two methods- Casual and Systematic.

(3) ***Correlation with practical life:*** According to Herbert Spencer the main aim of education is to prepare the students for future life. This aim can be achieved only if education is correlated with life. Therefore teaching of various subjects should be correlated with various aspects of life.

Correlation of the Teaching of Civics with Other Subjects

As a Social Science, Civics cannot be taught in isolation. Its teaching has to be correlated with the teaching of other subjects specially other social sciences.

Civics and Psychology

"Civics is a science which studies the conditions of the best possible social life". Life of man has to deal with various aspects of the society — social, economic, moral, political, religious, etc. All these facets of life make the human life ideal. It is not sufficient to develop only one aspect of the life of the individual. An attempt should be made to develop the various aspects of human life. Different subjects deal with different aspects of human life. Therefore, an attempt should be made to correlate the teaching of these various subjects. Prof. White has rightly remarked — "Civics is essentially a subject of connections, it links all time and periods as parts of the long chain of achievements beaten out of civilisations, it connects all subjects as part of the life story of mankind." Thus, Civics does not confine itself to the teaching of citizenship only. It should attempt to deal with the various aspects of human life.

Civics and Sociology

Sociology is the social science which studies various social relations of man. It studies the development of man as a social being. It studies economic, religious, moral and political developments of human society. Therefore, Civics forms a part of the study of Sociology.

Sociology deals with all the aspects of the social life of man, while Civics deals only with the civic aspect of the social life of an individual. It teaches men about their rights and duties as citizens. It also tells them about the ways and means through which political and social developments may be made. In short, Civics studies man only as a citizen while sociology studies man as a social being. Therefore teaching of these two social sciences is correlated. Their co-relationship is natural and beneficial.

Civics and History

History is the systematic study of the past events that have taken place in the society. It mirrors the social, political, economic and moral developments of mankind. The subject matter of Civics deals only with the civic life of an individual while History deals with all the aspects of human life in the past. It also presents before us the picture of the efforts made by human beings to reach the present stage of civilisation. Lord Sexton has rightly remarked- "The science of politics is the science that picks up the grains of gold from the sand of the river bed of history and forms a presentable ornament".

History is the study of the past while Civics is the study of the contemporary facts. In order to study the past we shall have to delve deep while for the study of the civics no such efforts are needed. Civics deals with various social and political problems as they affect the civic life of an individual.

The subject matter of History has a strong bearing on Civics. Man cannot make progress in the present unless he has an idea of the past. Civics draws on the funds of History to acquire knowledge of the past attempts of people in solving the various civic problems.

History and Civics were studied together for a very long time. Through the examples of History, the teacher of Civics can inculcate the qualities of discipline, patriotism, social services, etc, in the students. These qualities make a ideal citizen. Therefore, in order to become an ideal citizen one has to take advantage of the stock of History.

To quote Prof. Jones "History is a veritable mine of life experiences and the youth of today studies History that he may provide by the experiences of the race".

By the knowledge of History, a student of Civics can know the attitude of the past rulers towards citizens. He can also know the results of the attitude of the rulers. In the light of this knowledge a student of Civics can utilise the present day situations and bring about a good social and civic order.

Patriotism is an integral part of good citizenship. This trait can be developed in the students through the examples of great men of History. With the help of the examples of Shivaji and Maharana Pratap, the traits of chivalry and patriotism may be inculcated in the students and secularism may be developed through the example of Akbar. The example of Mahatma Gandhi shall inspire the students to make sacrifices, and live up to the ideals of truth and non-violence.

Thus, the knowledge of History is beneficial for the knowledge of Civics. Therefore, it is necessary to have horizontal correlationship between the teaching of Civics and History. Prof. Sealey has rightly remarked, "History without Civics has no root and: Civics without History bears no fruit".

Civics and Economics

Economics is the social science that studies various economic activities of men. It deals with the aspect of the society which describes about the production, distribution and exchange of the wealth. Wealth is very much needed for a happy and contented civic life. The knowledge of Economics helps the knowledge of civics. Thus, Economic efforts inspire people to make economics directed towards human welfare. Whether these efforts are moral or not moral is the concern of the Civics. Civics can teach people to behave in a reasonable and judicious manner with the labourers and the consumers.

The aim of Civics teaching is to inculcate the qualities of an ideal citizenship in the students. It aims at developing the society towards its goal. Such a development cannot be based on sheer ideal citizenship. It has to be based on the social wealth which alone can really bring about social welfare. Unless the economic condition of a society is good, economic development cannot take place. Thus, many things depend on Economics. With the present influence of Karl Marx on the thinking of the people, it has now been accepted that economics plays a vital role in the working of the society. Unless Economic relations are properly established, social and civic relations cannot be established properly. Thus, economic welfare is the basis of various developments- social cultural, moral, religious, aesthetic, etc.

Therefore we have to put in the element of Economics in the curriculum of Civics. Labour problems and the problems of the farmers and other members of the society are essentially economic problems. But they are also dealt with in Civics.

Economics and Civics are very much correlated. It has been rightly said, "Economics as an art depends on Civics and Civics as an art depends on Economics. They are supplementary and complementary to each other."

Civics and Geography

Man is the product of his geographical conditions. Various developments of the society, namely social, political, cultural, religious, moral, etc., are very much influenced by geographical factors. Way of living, culture, dress, etc., of people are in accordance with the geographical factors. Customs and traditions are influenced by the geographical conditions. People of temperate countries are hard working and their way of living is different from the people of the hot countries. Their culture is also different.

As Geography studies the natural problems of the world, therefore, it is natural for it to be correlated with Civics. With the help of the knowledge of geography students can have an idea about the culture and the way of living of the people of a country. Civics can take advantage of this knowledge.

Thus, although teaching of Civics and Geography is carried out independently of each other they are correlated. Both form part of the group of the social sciences known as social studies. Both aim at human welfare. Geography presents the background while civics can play on that background. The teacher of Civics should try to correlate the geographical factors with the teaching of the Civics. Taking advantage of the knowledge of the geographical factors can lay down rules and ways of making civic life happy. Both these sciences are correlated.

Civics and General Sciences

As General Science deals with the principles of the science it has very little to do with Civics. Under General Science comes the knowledge of the various factors of human life. Hygiene forms a part of General Science. Civics is indirectly related to General Science. The teaching of the two cannot be correlated directly.

Civics and Literature

Literature reflects social, economic, religious, political and moral problems of the society. It is the mirror of the society. The literary writer views the society from its own angle and tries to present it before its readers. The society may be improved through this knowledge.

Civics aims at developing ideal citizenship. It is based on certain ideals and values. The literary writer can inculcate these ideals and values in the young ones, without making them feel that certain things are being taught and presented to them as the ideals of human life. Literature can inculcate these ideals in the young students through indirect means.

Thus, the literary writer tries to teach the principles of Civics to the young students, in an indirect manner.

Various ideals of social life are reflected in various social sciences. If the teaching is conducted in a coordinated and correlated manner, the development of the personality is likely to be balanced and scientific. Correlation between the teaching of various subjects is helpful for the development of the personality of the students.

QUESTIONS

1. How would you correlate the teaching of Civics with the other subjects of the School Curriculum?
2. Discuss the correlation of Civics with Psychology, Sociology, History, Economics, Geography and General Sciences.

3. Indicate how you would correlate Civics with (a) Economics, and (b) General Sciences.

4. Discuss ways of correlating the teaching of Civics with other branches of social studies. State the limitations and possibilities in bringing out integration among these subjects.

17
Scene in India

Educational efforts can yield the expected results only if they are based on appropriate methods. Evidently, the problem of educational methods cannot be overemphasised. It includes some basic problems which are naturally in the way of the teacher's job in the school, certain difficulties and wrong ways of doing things in the class by the teacher, and what the teacher should do to remove these difficulties and wrong ways. The following are the factors underlying the problem of educational method :

Lack of Flexibility

Some teachers appear to be very rigid in the use of educational methods. They are not prepared to make any change in the method according to the demands of the situation. They follow the methods that they have been taught in the training college or that they have read in certain books. This helps them to finish the teaching of the subject-matter within the stipulated time limit, but it does not lead the student to acquire the fundamentals of the things taught. What is taught to them passes off their minds in due course.

It is difficult to recommend one single method of teaching that every teacher may follow. The teacher should be able to mould his methods according to the demands of the situation of the particular aspects of the subject-matter to be taught. The choice of a method depends upon the creative ability and progressive personality of the teacher. There should be a flexibility for introducing changes in method if the situation so demands. The teacher should feel free to incorporate the desired aspect of the various methods of teaching and forge out his own particular method. For example, by accepting the planning procedure of the Project Method, the specific aspects as defined in the Dalton Plan and the discussion aspect of the unit method, the teacher may be able to formulate his own method of teaching in accordance with the situational demands. However, the training college methods should be accepted as the fundamental structure on which the teacher has to reconstruct his own educational methods and procedures.

Multisided Process

Generally, the teacher alone is active in the class and the students remain sitting as passive listeners. It should be remembered that it is the student who has to be benefited from any educational effort. If he is not a participant in the educational procedure the very purpose of education is likely to be defeated. The objective of any educational method is to establish an organic relationship between the teacher and the taught and not only to impart information. Hence, teaching is a two-way process involving participation of both the teacher and the taught.

Functional Teaching Method

Thus, in the teaching process the student has to remain all the time active. He has to learn by doing and not only through cramming. Through learning by doing he will understand the practical implications of what he learns. He will be able to apply the same in his life situations as and when necessary. Therefore, it is said that the student should learn by living.

No Verbalism

Teachers who use numerous words in making a point, mistake words for information. In fact, there should be no verbalism in teaching method. The teacher should use minimum words in explaining a point. He has not to show that he can speak very fluently on any aspect. He should remember that he has not to establish his authority before the students, which is already recognised among the students. Therefore, the teacher has to see that acquisition of knowledge becomes functional in effect.

Regards to Individual Differences

There are individual differences in students. The students differ in their capacities, interests, aptitudes and abilities. Hence, the teacher has to adjust his teaching accordingly. If he does not do so, the brilliant and the dull both are likely to be ignored. There is no average student. The conception of average student is a myth. The teacher has to attend to individual differences found in students. He has to attend the more brilliant in some way. At other times he has to take care of the less privileged ones even in the group teaching procedure or afterwards. This will be possible through the active co-operation of the student. Each student should be given some special assignment according to his assets and limitations. Each student will acquire a functional attitude to adjust himself better in his environment. This will create in him a spirit of self-confidence, self-dependence and a sense of responsibility.

Enlarging the Students' Scope of Interests

There is a scope for the teacher to enlarge the interests of the students. Multi-sided interests enrich personality. The class-room,, the play-ground, excursions and cultural programmes are some of the occasions which may be utilized for enlargement of interests of students while teaching any subject. A clever and successful teacher never misses a single opportunity of developing his students' interests.

Developing Positive Attitudes and Good Character

The teacher is responsible for developing positive attitudes and marks of good character in students. He must stimulate the student to examine fully a particular situation at hand and then proceed further for its solution. This will develop in the student an attitude to look at things with an open mind. It will help him to adopt a liberal attitude towards various things in life. Hence, the method of teaching by the teachers should be directed towards influencing the student's total personality by way of developing his emotional and intellectual capacities, giving him a criterion for making right judgements and developing in him desirable values of life.

Practical Teaching

In the teaching process the teacher generally concentrates his efforts in helping the student learn certain informations, facts and the subject-matter of the course. This habit of teacher deprives the student from developing his faculties of discrimination, understanding of correlationship between things learnt, classifying things and teaching relevant conclusions. The method of teaching should be such as to facilitate the development of all these faculties.

The Burden of Home Work

Assigning home work without due consideration of the burden that the student might be carrying in other subjects retards the balanced development of students. Generally at the end of the period a teacher gives some home work. Thus, in various subjects the student is assigned some work. The total load becomes very heavy. Some students are able to do this home work somehow. Some others copy down the same from other student's note-book. As this home work is seldom examined by the teacher, the student is not adequately guided. He continues carrying wrong notions about many things. Hence, if any home work is given, that must be duly corrected, otherwise it will be better if the same is not given at all. The home work should be simple and small. It should be given according to a policy to be decided in consultation with other teachers. The major purpose of the home work should be to develop in the student a habit of self-study and to find out solutions of certain things which are within their reach. Therefore, the home work should be interesting, self-satisfying and stimulative.

No Spoon-feeding

The teacher has to develop the qualities of self-reliance, critical observation and judgement and self-control through his method of teaching. At times the teacher has to leave the student to himself to do things in the class, in experimental laboratories and in open fields and gardens. He must not fear that the student will make mistake. He should leave him free to learn things through his own practical experience so long as he does not harm himself physically. There is no harm in the experimental process if he breaks some implements, tools or equipment. Through so doing he is likely to develop his creative imagination which should be regarded the sole purpose of any method of teaching.

Problems of Teaching

As a subject the importance of Civics lies in its utility to the society. Though this importance has been recognised in India, but we are facing certain problems in civics teaching. Our educational system is such that a student of the subject gets only the theoretical knowledge of a subject, while, Civics is a subject which has its practical aspect. Even after more than fifty years of independence, India has not been able to give a practical shape to the theoretical knowledge acquired by students in the field of Civics.

Objectives of teaching are not clear: In Indian Schools, Civics is taught in such a way that the student is unable to know the real aim of the subject that he is studying. Different aims of teaching of Civics are development of character, development of sentiment of patriotism, development of mental power, consciousness about rights, etc. The real aim of Civics teaching is to build `man as man'. Ideal citizenship is the main aim of Civics. This aim is somewhat neglected in the teaching of Civics in Indian schools.

Defective curriculum: Some experts point out that the Curriculum of the Civics is defective in Indian schools. The teaching of Civics in Indian school starts at Junior High School classes. Too much emphasis is laid on the theoretical knowledge at this stage of study. The practical value of the Civics is more or less totally neglected. The case is almost the same in High School and Intermediate Classes. The curriculum of Civics is such that a student has to study the same topic from Junior High School stage upto Intermediate stage. The diversification of curriculum is totally neglected.

Inadequate aids: Teaching of Civics can be imparted in an appealing manner only if the teaching aids are utilized properly. However, in most of the Indian Schools, the teaching aids are not utilized. Only text-books and black-boards are available for the teaching of Civics while audio-visual aids like radio, film, script, tape-recorders, slides, projector and television even the -visual aids like model, lecture chart are absolutely not available. It goes without saying that teaching of Civics can not be effective when there are no proper teaching aids.

Defective teaching methods: In Indian Schools, the teaching of Civics is imparted only through text-book method and lecture method. Other methods of teaching such as observation method, project method, unit method and laboratory method are almost neglected. All these methods have their own importance in the teaching of Civics but due to lack of facilities and certain other reasons, Indian teachers do not teach Civics through all these methods.

Lack of proper arrangements: Civics is an almost neglected subject in Indian schools. There are no proper arrangements for its teaching. Upto Junior High School it is taught alongwith History and Geography. The result is that, the teacher lays more emphasis on Geography and History rather than Civics. There are no properly provided class-rooms for the teaching of Civics. The library facilities are absolutely inadequate.

Dearth of good Civics teachers: The teacher of Civics has an added value and importance in a democratic country like India, because he trains the students for ideal citizenship and in the democratic way of life. However, there is a great dearth of good Civics teachers in Indian schools. Available teachers have no faith in the teaching of the subject. If the teacher himself is not an ideal citizen how can he be expected to train the students in citizenship? If the teacher himself is not a democrat how can he be expected to train the students in the democratic way of life?

Defective system of examination: The systems of examinations and valuation are very defective in India. Much emphasis in laid on cramming. The system of essay type examination is prevalent in almost all the schools. Objective type of tests are rarely used. Generally it is believed that the written type of test or the essay type of examination is the correct method for assessing the achievement of the students. As Civics involves a lot of practical knowledge, it is necessary to devise some sort of practical examination to judge the attainment of the students in the subject. The students should be given an opportunity to take part in collective activities, organise work, parliaments, courts, assemblies and councils, etc. They should also be given an opportunity to learn the art of proper exercise of franchise. They should be given responsible positions in the field of games and other activities. This will provide them an opportunity for acquiring the traits of leadership.

QUESTIONS

1. "The teaching of Civics in Indian Schools is a difficult task." How far do you agree with this statement?

2. What are the problems of teaching of Civics in Indian Schools?